HERE COMES AMAZING YOU

49 Terrific Ideas for a Bigger, Better, Happier, Healthier, Sexier and MORE Vibrant Life Style!

CAROL SUE GERSHMAN

Disclaimer

This book is designed to provide information and motivation to the readers. It is sold with the understanding that the author or publisher is not engaged to render any type of psychological, legal, or any other kind of professional advice. If psychological, medical, or other expert assistance is needed, the services of a competent professional should be sought.

Every effort has been made to make this book as complete and accurate as possible. However, there might be mistakes, both typographical and in content. Therefore, this text should be used only as a general guide, and not as the ultimate source when it comes to change and transition or other areas with respect to personal development.

No warranties or guarantees are expressed or implied by the author or publisher to include any of the content in this book. Neither the publisher nor the author shall be liable for any physical, psychological, emotional, financial, or commercial damages, including, but not limited to, special, incidental, consequential, or other damages.

ISBN 978-0-9886999-0-8 - perfectbound
ISBN 978-0-9886999-1-5 - ePub
Library of Congress Control Number: 2012941250

Printed in the United States of America.

Dedication

DEDICATED TO THE AMAZING GIRLS AND
WOMEN IN MY FAMILY

LESLIE, EMILY, ALEX, SASHA, JUDY, TRACY, JOAN,
DARIA, ROBIN

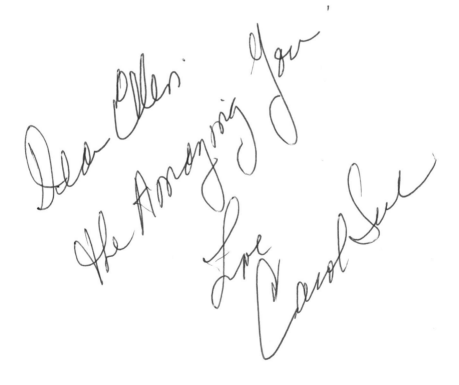

Suzanne Somers @SuzanneSomers

@CAROLGERSHMAN1 congratulations.
Keep up your good work

Acknowledgements

With loving thanks to Leslie Kuster, my wonderful daughter for her ongoing support.

With loving thanks to Eric Gershman, my smart son, for his valid critiques.

With love and thanks to my dear brother and sister-in law Mark and Joan for contribution on money chapter.

With love and thanks to my delightful sister Judy Davis for her advice on my cover design and much more.

Clara Solomon my dear friend, so many thanks and love for your incredible thoughts and passages.

With love and thanks to Janice Rockoff, my darling friend, for her listening ability.

Thank you David Rios, my pool lifeguard, for his one liner on education.

Thank you to Betty Wang Davis, executive shoe buyer at Saks 5th Avenue who took the time after giving birth to share her shoe expertise.

Many thanks to the brilliant internet contributors acknowledged throughout the book for their information and writings making research much easier.

Thank you Kelly Kios, my easy to work with editor.

Thank you to my beautiful granddaughter Emily for her writing on buying locally grown produce.

Thank you to my darling daughter-in-law Daria for a good recipe idea.

Thank you to all of the Mah Jongg Girls who stayed up nights trying to figure out the best title for the book.

Table of Contents

Part I: Your Inner Guide (Exploration)

Part 2: Your Health and Beauty

Part 3: Sex • Friendship • Money

Part 4: Enhancing Your Life

Part 5: Now Down to Basics

"Life is either a daring adventure or nothing."

— Helen Keller

Part I

Your Inner Guide (Exploration)

1

Imagination

How Deep Can You Go?

C an you imagine yourself free in spirit, living in the best of health and vibrancy, without paying any attention to how old you are? Can you imagine having more energy today than you had twenty-five years ago? You accomplish more, exercise more, eat more nourishing foods, drink pure water and get plenty of rest. You are no longer making the excuse, "If only it was ten years ago, maybe I could start a new business or take an extended trip or fulfill that impossible dream." Unfulfilled desires are no longer part of your life because you are living a full and upbeat life whether you are fifty, sixty, seventy or eighty plus.

The idea of what "old age" means has been ingrained into of all of us and most of us live according to societal norms and expectations. Some people start to die decades before their bodies actually go. Women start to die as their last child leaves home, men start to die when their careers end and they no longer have work. People feel lost when they lose their so-called identity: when the roles they have chosen come to their natural ending.

Sixty-five is the age our government chooses to send social security checks, but does that mean retirement? Why not retire at forty-five or ninety-five?

There are too many "supposed to do this" and "supposed to do thats!" These expectations cause much grief. Hanging on to those "shoulds" makes life so much harder than it needs to be. Whenever you catch yourself saying, "Should," it's a clue why you're in so much pain. Thinking the world should be a certain way is a waste of energy. It's the way it is.

Women are not supposed to go out by ourselves to a restaurant or a movie or travel alone because being alone is not supposed to be a good thing. When our children leave we are supposed to wait to have a grandchild, which makes us pressure our kids to have children so that we can be fulfilled again. We are supposed to live near our families or live with them as we age. Most of us are indoctrinated by our friends and families to follow the rules of society. When we are forty or fifty we are supposed to cut our hair and change the way we dress: no more minis or bikinis. Therefore, most people as they age will not venture outside their own comfort zone, thinking there is nothing new or exciting ahead.

When you catch yourself saying, should, ask yourself how you would feel about the situation if you simply dropped that word. Many times, just by doing that, you'll feel better about the situation. If we divorce we are supposed to go out and find a new spouse, and the sooner the better. We women are not supposed to be alone or independent. How many times have I heard an admirer say to me, "Why are you alone?" What an annoying, degrading question!

A friend once asked me, "What is good about old age? Nothing, she said." To me, there is only one thing that's **not** good about old age and that is getting closer to the inevitable. If we take care of ourselves and are blessed with good health, old age can be a wonderfully interesting period of life. We can get the answers to questions that might have frustrated us for a long time. Problems we thought insurmountable suddenly are no longer unsolved mysteries. We can create, love, live and teach others some of the tricks we have learned. We are living longer and healthier than any past generation and we are here to stay for a much longer stretch; living to one hundred is no longer a rarity. We can learn to live a more simple life.

So how do you imagine yourself at seventy? Sewing, sitting, saddening, medicating? Or do you expect to be vital, adventurous, beautiful, sexy, traveling, perhaps entering a new vocation or love affair? Whether it's to travel to a foreign country, learn a new skill or vocation, volunteer, or simply to spend time with family, the choice is up to you, and no one else. There are no "shoulds" anymore.

Scientists go to work each day and make new discoveries. They focus on giving us a longer life span; they test products and food so that we can be healthier and prolong our lives. We are living during amazing times.

We can begin new dreams at any age, new dreams that might take us down a path never realized. I still cannot believe I became a writer at seventy years old. A friend is getting married for the first time at age seventy. My own grandmother got married for the third time at eighty-two. We can go from grandma to hot lover in one night. Our parts work right into old age and yes, I will write about sex later in this book.

Why have any regrets at the end of your life about anything that you have not done? Step out of your conscious mind, just imagine and then do it!

So let's hurry up and get started. While I am not fond of exercises and there are no others in this book, this is one I use often that will help you get started on the journey to Amazing You.

SOME RECOMMENDATIONS FOR YOU:

- Close your eyes and simply imagine! Go deep into your imagination and keep a pencil and paper nearby. Try not to push any thoughts out of your mind. You may imagine a long road in front of you and on either side, two side roads. The side road on the left is where you can put whatever or whomever you no longer care to have in you life. On the road to the right, put new projects or people. Now pay attention to the road straight ahead. Does the road look wide and long or is there no road at all?

  When I do this exercise, if I see a shorter road, I quickly start to think about something new to expand the road. I want to always have a long straight road ahead of me with just a few curves to keep it interesting. Imagine! Go deep into your imagination and keep a pencil and paper nearby. Try not to push any thoughts out of your mind. When you open your eyes, look over your list and realize what came into your mind. Are you surprised at your thoughts? Now imagine doing everything on that list.

  Your age is a valuable commodity. You have years of wisdom because of your age, wisdom for yourself and to teach others. Let your age work for you not against you. If there is something you have kept yourself from doing or placed on the back burner, did it come when you closed your eyes and went into your imagination?

QUESTIONS FOR PERSONAL REFLECTION

1. Have you ever told yourself, "If it was only ten years ago, two years ago, I would have done this or that, but now it is too late." Can you imagine a new project, a diet, an exercise, a trip, falling in love, something you never thought could be possible happen to you now, without thinking too much time has passed on?
2. Could it be your lack of imagination that has held you back from being the full and vibrant you?
3. Does it seem impossible to think that anything different could happen in your life as you know it?
4. Did you enjoy thinking about the possibilities ahead of you?

As you can see you are limited only by your imagination!

Notes

2

Courage

Forget Those Fears and Roar Like a Lion!

Now that you have imagined doing something that has made you smile and dream, courage comes into play. I see it clearly now; it was only fear, lack of confidence and courage that stood in the way of practically any decision that I needed to make to move in a new direction. If you come from that dark place called fear, now is the time to recognize it and try to move forward on a path to a new and exciting life. Life is filled with many fears but when we allow them to rule our lives we might as well stay under the bed. The first step and the biggest step is to go out and find the courage to face your fears. Courage is relative. What is scary for some is a breeze for others.

People who live in the woods sometimes have fears of the city. The hustle, bustle, noise, masses of people and action frighten many. On the other hand some city folks have many fears about the woods. Animals, snakes, bugs, lack of services, few people, lost in the trees on an off beaten path. There are people who jump out of airplanes, bungee jump or run marathons. All of us have listened to reports about people who have shown courage beyond anyone's imagination and perhaps you are one of them. People get lost at sea for a week with no food or water, or stranded on a mountaintop in freezing temperatures, or those who stand up for a minority group against others when their life is at stake. The list goes on and on. Humans have an immense capacity for courage.

What about the courage it sometimes takes to get out of bed and start a new day when you are down? Sometimes finding the courage to continue day-to-day is as difficult as surviving on a mountaintop.

We develop courage as we experience life. Courage is the power of your will. To win what we want we need inner courage. We have to take risks and if we don't we will probably lose out.

For example, I was one of the first to arrive at the new phenomenon of South Beach, Florida. It was twenty-three blocks of unbelievable opportunities; you could not lose if you took the chance on a real estate investment. It was almost like winning the lottery. Who knew that it would turn out that way? There were many properties that I wanted to buy, but fear stepped in: "Suppose I lose, suppose the property goes down in value, suppose nobody will rent it." I brought my family down for support; they didn't see what I saw, my instincts were 100% correct, yet I backed out. Today I would have been a multimillionairess. In my profession, real estate investment, the pit in my stomach would begin when I was about to buy a new investment property. Now with time, when an opportunity comes my way, I am confident enough to know I am making the right decision. Age has its benefits.

Sometimes we become lazy, set in our ways, fearful of anything new or different. Traveling is a passion of mine. Going solo around the world with a backpack is a cinch to me yet others think I am courageous.

Yet there were many times, as the trip neared, staying home and feeling secure seemed the better choice. I would ask myself, "Do I really want to go? I am content here. It will be work and energy and decisions to make; I am comfortable at home." Then on the way to the airport I wondered why I ever would have chosen to stay home rather than experiencing life in every way within my possibilities.

Most of us have dealt with pain and loss. The end of a love affair causes incredible pain and it takes great courage to heal and fall in love again. I hope my kids have inherited their dad's courage. He can stand up tall after being knocked down. He stood up tall when he was fired as a stockbroker because of differences with his company; he went on to be a world-renowned photographer. He has since been challenged with many health issues but again has shown great courage in the process of healing. My daughter suffered five miscarriages. Each one was a tragedy and while I will never know the pain she suffered, she showed amazing courage as she healed from each one. She was put through another test of courage when the rowboat she and her boyfriend were in capsized one Thanksgiving Day on an icy lake. She kicked off her boots and said to herself, "I am not dying out here," swimming to shore chanting and praying. Her boyfriend, after calling out to her, "You are going the wrong way," drowned in the lake.

If you find yourself in an uncomfortable situation, lift up your chin and forge ahead. It is best to avoid dark lonely streets but if I find myself on one, I gather up courage by not running, simply walking with my head held high, eyes straight ahead almost as if the street belonged to me; how we want to go through life.

SOME RECOMMENDATIONS FOR YOU

"If only I had the courage." You do! Try to think about something that might take courage in different manner; maybe as simple as by letting go of others' opinions or trusting yourself that you are doing the right thing.

- Begin to develop courage to do some of the things you would like to do to live an ageless, passionate life.
- Courage takes only one thing. Doing it!
- Courage is what we need to do to make things right for ourselves.

QUESTIONS FOR PERSONAL REFLECTION:

1. How courageous have you been in your life? Have you awed your family and friends by your courage?
2. Were you ever in a situation when you needed courage but fear stepped in and you could not do it? Can you name your biggest fear? Can you go back and look into your history of why you developed such a fear?
3. What would it take for you to gather up courage to do something outside of your comfort zone ridding yourself of fear, accomplishing something you want to do?
4. Is there anything stopping you now from fulfilling a dream? Are you dismissing your own hopes dreams and creativity because of your lack of courage?

Do something that blows your mind before your next decade!

Notes

3

Self Esteem-Self Respect

It's Selling At Bargain Prices These Days!

Now that you have imagined a dream and found the courage to act upon it, self-esteem will come into play. People have a tough time enjoying their lives when they lack good self-esteem. Self esteem in about having an inferiority complex and ain't it a shame?

Posted on Nemours an internet educational site: "What is self-esteem? Yourself! You can't touch it, but it affects how you feel. You can't see it, but it's there when you look at yourself in the mirror. You can't hear it, but it's there every time you talk about yourself. Why is this important? It's how you see yourself and how you feel about your achievements. Good self-esteem is important because it helps you hold your head high and feel proud of yourself. It gives you the courage to try new things and the power to believe in yourself."

Some parents tell their kids they are beautiful and yet these kids go to school and hear it differently from their peers. They learn to self-judge harshly. They might not consider themselves good looking even if they truly are. Perhaps in class somebody laughed when you asked a question. Then at another time friends thought one of your ideas were foolish; something you tried to accomplish was not applauded; your self esteem hit rock bottom, so much so, that no matter what anyone tells you that is good about yourself, you carry the weight of not feeling that way. That is having low self-esteem. Then there is the opposite where parents abuse and put their children down and the kid grows up happy and well-adjusted with high regard and self-esteem. They think everything they do is great. It is tricky.

However, at this point of our lives, it is not about how we got there; we can no longer blame our parents or even our peers. It is where we are today and where we are going and the work we have to do on ourselves to build up our own self-esteem.

When I wrote my first book, it was necessary for me to give book talks. I worried, how could I ever stand in front of a group and speak? My daughter suggested I go to Toastmasters, a world wide organization focused on public speaking. Much to my amazement, there were doctors, lawyers, writers, people from all occupations who wanted to learn the skill of public speaking. At the first meeting I was asked to stand up, and state my name and why I came. My knees trembled and just that made my voice crack. Little by little the organization asked each one of us to stand up and each one was asked a question on a particular subject. Again my heart pounded and my voice quivered. After several months, I had to present my first speech and be evaluated on engaging the audience, how many "ums" I put into sentences, eye contact, standing tall. I studied for several months. When the time came for me to give my first book talk, I stood up and spoke clearly, with wit, humor and the audience had a great night and my self-esteem went right through the roof. You too can work toward confidence and better self-esteem. I had inherited that fear from my mom, who often said, "I could never in a million years speak in front of people." My mom liked to write poetry and I loved the poem she wrote at age 85. It began with: "I don't have space for more wrinkles on my face, but I am young." There was something about that line that grabbed me. Soon after I heard about a poetry contest in California. My mom would have the opportunity to recite her poem and possibly win an award. My sister and I brought her to the Poet Laureates convention. When it was time for her to get up and recite her poem, I was a nervous wreck, much like I'd felt when my kids got up to do something. I trembled at the thought of her missing her lines, but she was perfect. She loved it and hardly wanted to get off of the stage. She was given the opportunity to get over her lifetime fear and her self-esteem skyrocketed. She could hardly believe what she had accomplished. That is usually all it takes, Doing it!

According to *Psychology Today*, "The person with self-respect simply likes her or himself. This self-respect is not contingent on success because there are always failures to contend with. Neither is it a result of comparing ourselves with others because there is always someone better or worse. These are tactics usually employed to increase self-esteem. Self-respect, however, is a given. We simply like ourselves or we don't. With self-respect, we like ourselves because of who we are and not because of what we can or cannot do. Life is joyous when we like ourselves. We don't allow others to abuse or hurt us and if they do it hardly will effect us because we are proud of who we are and that builds our self esteem."

SOME RECOMMENDATIONS FOR YOU

- Have you ever looked at yourself in the mirror and said, "I love you?" You might feel silly but tomorrow I would like to see you get up and brush your teeth and before doing anything else, say, "I love you" out loud. The more you do it the more you will feel love for yourself which of course will effect how you eat, exercise, dress, function and live a happier life.

- Having good self-esteem is also the ticket to making good choices about your mind and body. If you think you're important, you'll be less likely to follow the crowd if your friends are doing something dumb or dangerous. If you have good self-esteem, you know that you're wise enough to make your own decisions.

- Value your whole self! Every part of you is worth caring for and protecting.

- Self-esteem isn't bragging about how great you are. It's more like quietly knowing that you're worth a lot (priceless, in fact) It's not about thinking you're perfect — because nobody is — but knowing that you're worthy of being loved and accepted. Don't we have the concept that it is important to accept our limitations? As the Serenity Prayer by Reinhold Neiburh states: "God grant me the serenity to accept the things I cannot change; courage to change the things I can; and wisdom to know the difference."

QUESTIONS FOR PERSONAL REFLECTION:

1. How do you feel when you walk into a room of strangers?
2. How do you feel when you walk into a room with friends?
3. When you receive a compliment, do you brush it off, thinking you are not worthy of receiving it?
4. Is self-esteem something you feel you have always lacked, admiring those who have it?
5. By drawing someone else out, you might bring yourself out increasing your self-esteem. Will you give it a try?

Like yourself, love yourself.
It is the key to true
happiness!

Notes

4

Independence

Do You Prefer Leaning on Someone's Shoulder? You Might be a Heavy Load!

Independence Day, July 4th is one our most spectacular American holidays. Signing the Declaration of Independence freed our country and we have been celebrating this freedom ever since. When we are in control of taking care of ourselves, not dependent on another for survival, we have achieved our own independence. For a woman holding on to a man's arm, being chauffeured and escorted might feel good, but a woman must also know how to stand alone. It is best that she knows what she wants and prepared to take care of herself as well. We women of a certain generation grew up in our parents' home and then went straight into marriage. We were given budgets, allowances, and rules from our husbands. When I was a new bride, a friend confided that her mom taught her to always put a little money away for herself. I thought that was the most deceitful thing I ever heard. Back then, I was far from an independent thinker. My only independence was present in my kitchen, cleaning and taking care of our kids. One of my friends filled with the kind of talent that would have brought her Broadway fame stopped studying because her husband forbid her to follow her star. She accepted this as part of marriage because marriage was more important to her than a career. While I came from a family of women who worked, I did not. Very few of my friends did, either.

One day, our generation began to wake up. We began to separate ourselves from our partners quickly becoming the guinea pigs of the divorce era, caught up in women's liberation. Spouses had a hard time dealing with the changes in their wives; wives had a hard time with their husbands, many of whom on both sides began to have love affairs. Out of eleven couple friends in our circle, only one remained married. Women began to live alone with their kids as the husbands one by one began to move out.

Some of us did not know how to write a check, or go anywhere on our own. Finally, I decided to go into business. Pulling my car out of the driveway and going to work became my favorite part of the day. Earning enough money to take a summer place with my son was thrilling.

Independence means free from the influence, guidance, or control of another or others. To be self-reliant is to have an independent mind. It felt magnificent.

Times have changed. Now it is a rare woman who does not work, women juggling both careers and home lives. Nannies now do the cooking, cleaning and child rearing while moms go out to work. Day care centers are more popular than ever.

Some of us now have become so independent that it is difficult to find a mate. Putting up with the habits or the needs of another person might well now be avoided; we detest snoring and all the rest of the habits that goes with each of us. We independents have become set in our ways and don't want dependency. Men had to go through their changes, accepting their woman will have a career. They too had to change and are still being threatened by the woman who goes out in the world and who might earn more money than he.

Michael Taylor, (author of *The Online Friend*), states: "All of this is good because it means our society has become less rigid and we have been able to take advantage of the many ways to live an independent life, even if we are married. We needed this change. Making your own money is a great thing even if it means living a lesser life style. You know you can stand alone. Being independent does not mean living a solitary life and never asking for help."

There are men who still prefer a woman who is dependent on them and some women only know how to live being dependent on a man. For those who still prefer not to be independent preferring to hang on or cling to another person being protected and tucked in at night that man is waiting to take care of you. Some men and women don't mind being a burden to a family or others. Some parents, guardians or partners enjoy being needed, but ultimately inappropriate dependency is draining, burdensome, and forms an unhealthy, unbalanced relationship.

There is a woman who needs a cane but her self image does not allow her to use one. She would prefer to hang on the arm of her husband or friends weighing them down.

23

SOME RECOMMENDATIONS FOR YOU:

- For those of you who feel your lack of independence, give yourself your own Independence Day. Allow yourself to do the things you want to do without asking permission.

- Know that if you lose your spouse you will be able to carry on, that you will know how to take care of your finances, health, transportation to name a few.

- There may come a time that it will be impossible to take care of yourself, a day that most will dread, so start practicing now to do what you dream of before it is too late.

QUESTIONS FOR PERSONAL REFLECTION:

1. How are you faring these days? Are you dependent on someone or too independent not able to share your life with anyone?
2. Do you prefer to have someone take care of you? If not your spouse, perhaps your children? Do you burden your children by being fearful of doing things on your own?
3. Have you taught your children to be independent allowing them to make their own mistakes?
4. Do you constantly ask others opinions before you make a move?

Sign your own Declaration of Independence today!

Notes

5

Loneliness

It Happens To The Best Of Us!

When I first separated from my husband, a new friend paid me a visit. "Loneliness is a big business," she said, words I've never forgotten. At the time it was unclear to me what she meant but learned quickly how right she was. There is a world of lonely people out there, both married and single, and we wonder why they are the perfect targets for a scam. Loneliness is about feeling isolated, unattached and empty. Loneliness within a marriage or a relationship is one of the worst of the lonely feelings because of being trapped in the relationship as well. When communication and sex has ceased from what was once a loving caring relationship, loneliness becomes extremely painful. Loneliness can bring on many things for you to combat. You might start buying friendships, paying for a friend to go out to dinner with or buying unnecessary gifts for someone else or yourself, shopping excessively to fulfill your lonely needs. A lonely person might commit to someone they do not love, invite people to their home who are only there to eat their food and drink their wine without reciprocation, using you. The lonely might play the TV all day long just to have other voices in the room.

Men seem to have a much harder time adjusting to being alone than women. Most men, after a breakup, will seek a new partner quickly. We have all heard the many stories of a spouse losing their long term partner and passing away soon after. While their children may be caring, they might still feel alone and isolated within their own children's home or living nearby. This is why it is important to keep up hobbies building self-esteem and self-confidence to the point that you thoroughly enjoy your aloneness and your own company. Jails are said to be the worst punishment because of the isolation one must endure.

Are you lonely? Don't worry—most people are from time to time. People need other people no matter how independent they are. Perhaps you have brought loneliness on to yourself by living in an isolated area even though some people find small towns easier to connect with others as the people might be friendlier. When a home is bustling with children living in a rural area works, but when the house is emptied it is probably best to live in a more urban area. Then again it is said that cities can be even more isolating if you are alone, although walking outside into city life where there are movie theaters, parks, restaurants and museum to spend time surely will make you feel less isolated and lonely. Simply knowing there is life outside is comforting. The point being isolating yourself if you live alone or at any time, can cause great loneliness and emptiness. No matter, we need to reach out to other people and have our own interests.

One of the hardest aspects of loneliness is that people will not seek you out. One has to pursue the company of others and it might not be an easy thing to do as rejection might be waiting for you. It can be hard to enter an established group of friends. But the lonely must keep trying to protect their mental health. It only takes one person to bring joy and happiness to you. Go out and talk to a stranger, smile at someone. Even if they don't initially engage with you, keep sending out positive vibes. Some people are not used to friendliness. Reach out to people until you find companionship.

What we know as the lonely hearts club has expanded to on line dating and millions have joined the various sites hoping to find a companion, a mate, a friend (more on this topic later in the book). With the Internet at our fingertips, there are hundreds of meetup groups for everybody. All you need do is Google meetups in your city and put in your request. This is a good thing. Loneliness is curable.

SOME RECOMMENDATIONS FOR YOU

- Become interested in something new, almost anything you might enjoy.

- Become more interesting by reading or taking a class. Try many different classes. Some let you sit in for the first session to see if it works. Find an inspiring teacher who will pique your interest and make you think.

- Buy a series ticket, so you always have something to look forward to. For that matter, plan something to look forward to doing, even if it is months away. Buy a new outfit for that new occasion.

- Join your local Y or religious organization. There are many classes and events to attend. Friendships are built through familiarity, so seeing the same group of people over time will breed relationships.

QUESTIONS FOR PERSONAL REFLECTION

1. Have you experienced terrible loneliness?
2. What did you do to combat it? What are you doing to combat it now?
3. If you were in a lonely relationship, were you able to find a better lifestyle by leaving your mate?

Seek out others.
They would love your
company and friendship!

Notes

6

Mistakes, Failure And Regrets

Make More Mistakes, Fail More, Regret Nothing!

The more mistakes you make in life the more you can learn about yourself. The only big mistake you could make is not learning by them. There are some of us who have to make the same mistakes repeatedly to learn our lessons; sometimes it can take a lifetime. Some never learn. There are all kinds of mistakes. Some are permanent mistakes or failures; many are lost opportunities and those are the ones we regret the most. If one needs to repeat their learning lessons till they get it, it might take some time. People can attach themselves to their mistakes and don't move forward living by their past behavior instead of accepting learning and moving on. I have made many mistakes and probably will keep on making them because I am human. Someone once said, "I wish I had made more mistakes." Making new ones and learning new lessons can be beneficial. Today hitting the curb hard when I parked my car caused damage to the fender. Does that mean I am a failure? Certainly I was able to safely drive there and back well. It was a careless mistake but did not make me feel like a failure. Perhaps curb hitting will be out of my life for good.

Do your best to appreciate the risks and opportunities you have taken, no matter the outcome; to look at it in a different way there are no mistakes. Every mistake we make is a learning experience and a lesson bringing our spirit to a higher plateau. Nobody is perfect.

Failure and mistakes are not the same thing:

According to Kevine Ikenberry, Leadership Expert, Speaker, Consultant, Author, Trainer, "Failure is something that occurs over time. We all can think of mistakes we have made that we learned from, that become incredibly important in our growth and development, and are far from being failures, because they contributed to our success. As human beings, this is not likely our best thought process. I suggest we remember the difference between mistakes and failure, and realize that when we focus on our mistakes as an opportunity to learn, we are much more likely to not experience failure over the longer term. I believe that people often label themselves as failures (if only subconsciously) when they make a mistake."

Regrets tend to stay with us even when we replace them with an accomplishment. We might still say, " Don't you remember when **that** happened etc?" It is about self esteem and thinking enough of yourself to know that you tried something or didn't try something and if another opportunity comes your way you will look upon it differently. Human beings have the most difficulty in forgiving their own selves. We need to get past that way of thinking. There are always new opportunities, even though it might not be the one you thought it would be.

"In order to get mentally and emotionally past previous regrets seize present opportunities. In order not to have any farther regrets do the things you dream about doing, take action, do not procrastinate."

There were those wonderful real estate deals that would have put me over the top wealthy; involvements in a love relationship and the mistakes that drove him away. Did I have lost opportunities? "Yes," Regrets? "No." People can see their marriages as failures. But why is this, as long as you married for love? Emotions change; we outgrow one another; we learn from each other even if the outcome was not what we thought it would be; we may have children or more security from knowing that person. What is there to regret? Did you think you were secure for life by always being married? The only real security there is lies within each of us.

QUESTIONS FOR PERSONAL REFLECTION

1. We all fail at something. In the end, what does it really mean, as long as we do not keep dwelling in the past or allow it to ruin the rest of our lives. What do you think of your personal failures, if any? Are you still dwelling?
2. Did you go on to do something bigger and better than you ever thought possible?
3. What was the most memorable mistake you ever made? How did it turn out? Did you learn from it without repeating the same mistake or did it take many tries?

Respect yourself, even when you make mistakes. When you respect yourself, others will respect you too!

Notes

7

The Wasted Emotions:

Guilt, Worry, Obsession!

If you are Jewish you are guilty.

That is a joke amongst Jewish people even though many other cultures have plenty of guilt complexes.

"Maybe I should **have** done that"

"Maybe I should **not** have done that."

"Maybe I should **have** said that."

"Maybe I should **not** have said that."

"Maybe it **wasn't** enough."

"Maybe it *was* too much."

"Maybe It was the **wrong** thing to say."

"Maybe it was the **right** thing to say even though it might have been the wrong thing to say."

Guilt often comes from trying to avoid a situation; something you think you should have done and now you feel you let the other person down or yourself down. You don't want people to be angry at you, you don't want to let someone down, you don't want people to be upset. Maybe you will pass up a good opportunity because you are afraid of the outcome and you might feel guilty. Some people feel guilty when they avoid doing something that they think they should have done like disappointing your parents, your family, your friend or poor performance on a job.

I was on the television show *The Price Is Right*. I was the big winner and was asked back the next week. I was winning so much again that second week that I suddenly felt guilty knowing all the answers. I blew the last product. Go figure!

While I was the one taking my mom to her doctor appointments and watching over her, after she passed way, I felt guilty that I hadn't done enough. Guilty thoughts flooded my mind: what about that time I yelled at her or didn't come that day? I have never acted perfectly so why would I have expected her to think I had suddenly become perfect? Yet, the guilt is with me today. All the good deeds I performed have been wiped out with guilt.

You will come across people who are absolute experts at making you feel guilty; they have figured you out. My ex-husband would wake me up in early morning in the freezing cold to go skiing with the family. When I did not get out of bed, I felt guilty. "I should have gone, why didn't I get up, I missed the fun, he won't admire me, the kids would have liked me to come, I did the wrong thing by staying in bed," I told myself. Guilt, Guilt, Guilt. Didn't I know enough about me to know it was not something I wanted to do?

According to Catherine Pratt's "Dealing With Feeling Guilty," learning how to deal with guilt comes down to understanding what's really happening behind your feelings of guilt. Once you do that, then you take control over your emotions and you choose how you want to respond. You won't be blindly reacting and finding that nothing you do eases your guilty conscience. This way, you rule your life, not your emotions and fear. You're also back to making the best decisions for you and those you interact with."

QUESTIONS FOR SELF REFLECTION

1. In general how guilty do you feel?
2. Can you accept yourself as you are and not feel guilty even if you do something against someone you love?
3. Have you reached a point in life when you can say,"NO" and be proud of yourself for saying it and not guilty?"
4. It might take a lot more work and therapy could be needed for those that cannot overcome their guilt. Have you gone that route?

Try to make guiltless decisions!

Notes

8

Worries

Do You Have Any? Many?

Do any one of these sound familiar?
- I worry about my children, they didn't answer the phone today, so what if they are 54 years old?

- I worry about terrorists killing others, killing me.

- I worry about traveling on an airplane. I worry they will lose my bags.

- I worry about disasters; hurricanes, tornadoes, suppose the ocean goes into tsunami and earth is wiped about.

- I worry about my health; I had too many colds this year, my stomach hurts, maybe it is cancer.

- I worry about my money, I worry about being robbed.

- I worry about walking down the street after dark.

- I worry about my grandkids and how my kids are bringing them up.

- I worry about my hair losing body and worry about the new line on my face.
- I worry when my kids take a plane on vacation; better they should stay home.
- I worry about the plane when I go on vacation, I worry about the cruise ship germs so I won't cruise.

When it comes to worries, I have heard them all, including my own. So what is worry and why do we do it even if there is absolutely nothing we can do about it?

Everyone worries to some extent. It could be about something little, like what you think you got on a test, or something big, like major surgery. We worry because we fear. Parents who have suffered terrible losses might worry that much more about their other children. We are all aware of the terrible things that could happen to a person. If you don't hear from your loved ones you begin to worry, could that be happening to them? Driving and late, automatically goes into a car crash mode. Sometimes worry can work in a way of being forewarned. My daughter was once taking a flight to an important business meeting. I had a terrible dream that the worst would happen. At first I did not want to tell her about my dream, but then I thought suppose something did happen and here I was forewarned. So I told her. Even though for me it would have been a difficult decision, she was not worried. "Mom, there is nothing in my life that tells me not to take the flight."

Do you worry so much that you worry about worrying too much? In the end, if you just worry about what's going to happen tomorrow, when will you have the time to live today?

SOME RECOMMENDATIONS FOR YOU

- The best way to stop worrying is to live in the moment. Pay attention to yourself and each activity you do. For example, if you are reading this, there is no room to think about anything else other than what you are reading. Living in the moment is the only true way to live and when you do you will experience your life fully and not be interrupted by worries.

- I learned a good lesson about flying after 9/11. After the bravery showed by the people on the planes that were hit, I needed to learn to be as brave as they were, and not act like a fearful child when flying. Therefore now, I mosey to the airport, take my seat, pick up a book or such sit back and enjoy the flight. I no longer worry as nothing could have been more horrific than what they went through. If there is nothing to worry about, why worry that there will be? Any landing is good as long as it is a safe landing.

- *Wikihow on internet* suggests the following thoughts on worrying:

- Realize that you can't stop the bad things, so you might as well focus your mind on the positive.

- Perhaps you need to learn to be comfortable with risk. There are simply no guarantees in life, and nearly everything carries some level of risk. Also, if something bad has happened to you in the past, it becomes worrisome not to have it happen again, still none of your endless worrying will help to prevent it, so live in the moment and enjoy your life.

- Are you trying to save the world? If you feel like it's your job or responsibility to stop bad things from happening (perhaps to your family, your business, or at all), you're placing too much pressure on yourself. You may have a hero complex. You're only human, and to set yourself an unattainable standard will only cause pain and disappointment.

- Take action by doing what you are worrying about.

  Dr. Wayne W. Dyer, internationally renowned author and speaker states:

  "Worry is a technique you created to fill the moments of your life. What is worry, he asks? Worry is the act of becoming immobilized in the present moment as a result of things that are going, or are not going, to happen in the future."

  What Dr. Dyer is suggesting is that we might use worry to stop living in the present, instead, using them to fill your time by worrying. A worrier remains inactive caught up in their worries immobilized do anything else but worry. Examine all the things you worry about today and remind yourself that in 15 years, all you will have done with your worry-mind is avoided living fully in your present moments'

  Worrying is destructive to us in many ways. It becomes a mental burden that can even cause us to grow physically sick.

QUESTIONS FOR SELF-REFECTION

1. Are you that worrywart? Why?
2. Are you the mother who makes your kids call you even when they are on vacations so YOU don't worry? Can you not live and let live and trust?
3. Do you think letting your children know that you worry about them brings them comfort?
4. Has your worrying proved anything new to you that if you would not have worried it would have had a different outcome?
5. Have you saved anyone from their worries?
6. What have all of your worries brought to you? Did you solve the problem, is your life any better for worrying?

Now have you stopped worrying?

Notes

9

Obsession

If You Had It At 14 You Will Have It At 70!

Obsession is a persistent disturbing preoccupation that does not leave the head. I must admit I have carried the bug starting at age fourteen. In my last book, *The Jewish Lady, The Black Man And The Road Trip*, I took all of my negative thoughts and obsessions about the break up and put them into writing. Much like worry, obsession makes no sense whatsoever, yet it can occupy your mind and life causing you to put your real life aside. Obsessions are involuntary, seemingly uncontrollable thoughts, images, or impulses that occur repeatedly in your mind. You don't want to have these ideas but you can't stop them. Unfortunately, these obsessive thoughts are often disturbing and distracting. Nobody can talk you out of it. In the case of love, you might replace one obsession with another but not until you finally say enough is enough will your obsessing cease. It can be over in one minute by just stopping BUT ONLY IF YOU WANT TO.

Stalkers are obsessed people who interfere with the lives of others. Obsession forces you to do outrageous unreasonable things. The obsession is so intense that nothing other than object of the obsession exists. An obsessed person will not be able to move on to someone or something new while they are obsessing about something else. Romantic obsession creates an illusion: that one can find happiness from another person.

Then there are those who cannot leave the house, mop their floors ten times a day. Check their e-mails every five minutes, call their mates twelve times a day, thinking they may be having an affair. An obsession can also be labeled as good company as it can keep you from being lonely as your mind is always occupied. An obsession can keep you from achieving goals allowing you to start new things.

SOME RECOMMENDATIONS FOR YOU

- Go for help to a therapist and discuss with the therapist how much time you are spending obsessing.
- Don't be surprised if it does not help.
- Try to replace the object you are obsessed with something to occupy your mind in another way.
- Give it time, but know you will be cheating your own self out of living because what you are doing is completely unnecessary.
- If you are obsessed you are focused on your obsession as time rolls away.

QUESTIONS FOR SELF REFLECTION

1. Do you obsess, where you become fixated on something that you don't have and won't let it go?
2. Has your obsession kept you from living in the moment and enjoying your life?
3. Do you enjoy your obsession because it keeps you occupied and not lonely?

Obsession, just like a Fantasy, can keep you from loneliness because you carry them with you all the time!

Notes

How NOT to be the
amazing you

10

Gossipy Angry and Rude?

Let's Not Be!

Are you a **gossiping** meanie who loves to open your mouth and tell the secrets of others? Hmmmmmmm? You may not think you have a big mouth, or that you are saying anything out of line, yet who would ever have known that piece of gossip if you didn't share it?

Or do you think you are simply entertaining people by revealing some nasties about another simply to get a big WOW?

Before you speak ask yourself: Is what I'm about to say true? Is it necessary? Is it kind? Are you spreading something that you only have imagined or dreamed up? Are you helping the other person by speaking your words or just needful to make a juicy splash.

The person who you are addressing reaction might be shock or that might say, " I knew it all the time."

If they knew it all the time, they've kept their big mouth shut, so why haven't you?

Are you the person who wants to spread the bad news first?

"Aunti Tillie died; did you hear who is in the hospital; guess what? Saw John out with another woman; I guess their marriage isn't that great, after all."

While it is rewarding to have a confidant who we are able to tell what is on our minds and be our gossipy selves, it is essential to choose a confidant you can trust not to repeat your words, start rumors or harm to someone. People like to talk and you might find yourself stunned one day to find that someone you completely trusted passed on your secretive news. Choose carefully and be grateful when you do have a confidant. There is no harm in talking about yourself, that is, if you have a couple of good listeners around.

No question my divorce was caused by one **angry** soul. She could ask mind-blowing questions of naive thirty year old me, putting nasty thoughts into my innocent vulnerable head.

"Do you really think you have a good marriage?"

"Of course I do."

"Your husband doesn't pay much attention to you."

"Really? You don't think so?"

I realized she might be right, so I became skeptical and started to watch his ways. She not only aided in breaking up my marriage but she was able to successfully break up two other marriages. She had a gift to go into that deep dark place we feared to recognize on our own. All three of us were young and vulnerable and later divorced, and supported all the way by her. Don't let yourself become a person who ruins the lives of others. It brings no one happiness—not even you.

If you know that you are an angry person and that it doesn't take too much to set you off, try to go for help. There are many anger management programs. Some folks have ability to hide their anger by taking it out in other ways, such as road rage or an unexpected outburst of anger. There is plenty of help out there if you just ask for it. A mean person is disrespectful to other people. They are harsh with their words and actions and they are able to abuse others with their spiteful ways.

And then there are the **"rudies."** They seem unable or unwilling to align their behavior with laws known to the general population of what is socially acceptable. The **"rudies"** are the usually at their worst in a restaurant, treating the waiter disrespectfully. I guess they think they are paying for their service so therefore it is their privilege. Can you imagine how many times their food is spit into? **"Rudies"** show up in other ways. They are into their own selves, they hardly listen to another person when they are speaking and think nothing of interrupting when the speaker is in the middle of a sentence. Another way a **rudie** struts their stuff if by being notoriously late or keeping other people waiting at every given chance. They have no consideration for others and while they can be sensitive people in some instances, they treat others with great insensitivity. The only thing that could help this person is good discipline; if it is too late for mother than a spouse can whip their **rudie** into shape.

When you are rude you distinguish yourself as being void of social class, presenting yourself as the only person of any importance. Being rude is a terrible trait and you place your reputation at stake by being one. People who have accomplished major tasks in their lives are humble quiet and polite with good manners. Stand in line at a Kmart or a Walmart where the masses shop and you will see polite people, kind to one another and when a **rudie** comes into the line people are taken aback by snarling or laughing. Certainly if you are looking to stand out or be noticed, you can accomplish that by being rude. Try to practice being polite. Listen, express thanks and most important show patience.

SOME RECOMMENDATIONS FOR YOU

- Don't engage in backstabbing gossip

- Be careful of the people who gossip to you, because you can be sure they are talking just as loudly about you.

- Be nice, be kind and try to listen. Silence is a wonderful thing but for some the hardest thing to do.

- Catch yourself the next time you are being rude. Think how you must sound and look to the people around you. Is this how you want to live your life? Think instead about becoming Amazing New You.

QUESTIONS FOR SELF REFLECTION

1. Can you admit that you are a gossip?
2. How do you feel about people who tell you stories about others that are disrespectful or talk behind their backs? Think how you would feel if that person treated you in that manner.
3. Have you ever considered yourself rude?
4. Are you showing you have no regard for people or are you showing you have no regard for yourself?
5. What does being rude do for you? How do you think you are making the other person feel?
6. Ask yourself where and why did you learn to be rude and what gives you that right?

As the saying goes, "if you don't have something nice to say, why say it?"

Notes

Back on the right track to becoming the amazing you

11

Apology

Me Wrong? When?

W hy do people find it so hard to apologize even when they are guilty? It takes so little to set the record straight and yet people have difficulty admitting they might have done something wrong.

There are people who do know when they are wrong, and there are also times when we are not aware of our mistakes and suddenly find someone missing from our lives. If you go back in time you might get what Oprah calls an "aha moment." It happened to me. A friend called me at an inopportune moment. It bothered me because she knew I was doing something important that day, so I abruptly hung up on her. After realizing I had not heard from her in some time, I put two and two together calling to apologize and our friendship went on for many years. However, in my heart of hearts I did not believe she ever truly forgave me and would often kid her about it. As it turned out at least forty-seven years later to the day we had another disagreement. She felt hurt because I found it necessary to postpone my visit till the next day. I humbly apologized which was not accepted and I realized she was down right mean. She did not want to accept my apology. Wouldn't it have been that much more magnanimous to accept it and move on? We have since parted ways, proving she had been upset for 47 years.

SOME RECOMMENDATIONS FOR YOU

- Apologies are necessary when you know that you made a mistake and care for the person enough to set the record straight.

- Be sincere and show that you are truly sorry by not allowing the person to have any doubt of how sorry you are. Perhaps your might state how important that person is to you and how void it would be without having them in your life. Now is the time to be humble and sincere trying to repair your relationship with the person.

- When you make an apology, no "buts" should be added. "I am sorry, but" is a no-no. Another no-no, "I am sorry you feel that way." You should be sorry for making them feel that way.

- "Please forgive me" is asking the other person to forgive you, but you have forgotten the apology.

- "I am sorry, won't you please forgive me?" is a good start.

- Leaving a voice mail message or sending a text is **not** a proper way to apologize. However, following up with a phone call can help the situation.

- What is the worst apology you have ever received? For me it was when opening my heart to someone about their wrong doings to me, their response was, "Sorry you feel that way but that is the way it is." Even if you feel strongly about what you've done, try to sympathize with the other person's pain and further explain your need. You very well might lose that person to accomplish your goal so decide which is more important.

- Being late is being rude and it deserves an apology. If you say meet at seven, be there at seven. You are keeping someone waiting on their time giving you power over them.

- Be careful about important dates and remembering them so you will not have to apologize for forgetting them.

- Be careful of the promises you make. This is disappointing to another person if you fail to keep them. Or you will quickly get a bad reputation for not keeping your promises and destroying trust.

- Be kind. If you sincerely hurt someone and they accept your apology, be grateful. Some people prefer to stay angry even though you may apologize. There's nothing you can do to make someone forgive you.

- Forgiveness is as important as an apology. It takes a big person to accept an apology if they have been badly hurt.

- Once you make the apology and it has been accepted, do not rehash what happened. It's in the past now.

- Apologies are humbling and good for your soul so hurry and apologize if you are in the wrong.

QUESTIONS FOR SELF-REFECTION

1. Is making an apology hard for you to do?
2. When you receive an apology that is sincere, are you able to forgive and forget?
3. Have you accepted the apology but have gone on disliking that person and never truly forgiven them?

Wouldn't it be wonderful to live life never explaining or apologizing because you have lived it with integrity and kindness?

Notes

12

Integrity And Loyalty

What Are Your Intentions Young Man?

"What are your intentions, young man?" is a more profound question than we might believe. Both man and woman can proclaim their love, yet at any given moment, they can shut down and turn away showing a lack of integrity with no remorse, never looking back.

According to *Dr. Margaret Paul, author, counselor, therapist, copied from internet April 28, 2008*: "As long as people operate under the false belief that happiness lies in getting what they want externally, rather than in whom they choose to be in the world, they will be lacking integrity on their way to getting what they think they want. People who lack integrity will lie, steal, throw tantrums, say anything that comes into their head at the moment to get what they want without any regard for others. Their only focus is getting what they want at that very moment."

Unfortunately, we probably know people who do not possess that wonderful attribute called integrity; the people who do not care about other people as long as their own satisfactions are met. Integrity is our heart. They might justify their behavior, but the truth is, they lack integrity. "They could have fooled me." These are the people to watch out for in life. Integrity is defined as "having moral principles, honesty, wholeness and unity within your own being."

A person with integrity might not always do the right thing, but their heart is in the right place and if things do not work out, you will be able to understand why. What is life without integrity? What does trusting someone mean? Think about the Ponzi schemes for their own glutton. If you buy a vanilla ice cream cone you want it to taste like vanilla: the same with a person. If you trust or love a person you want them to be who they say they are; things might not work out between people but you have lived the truth. People with integrity are honest, authentic and we can trust them.

I wondered what the difference was between loyalty and integrity and got my answer. I found the answer on Ask.com According to Katherin A:

"Loyalty, is faithfulness or a devotion to a person, country, group, or cause. Integrity is a concept of consistency of actions, values, methods, measures, principles, expectations and outcomes. Integrity is our own personal honesty."

SOME RECOMMENDATIONS FOR YOU

- Be careful or at least think about the person you are getting involved with. Most people are wonderful but check it out anyway. Many times people tell you up front who they are, but we tend not to believe them. If a person tells you something negative about themselves, believe them. Live your life trusting but being aware that other people can pull the wool over your eyes. There are those who will try to get away with whatever they can especially if you are a vulnerable person.

- Build your own character to a higher quality. Learn how by learning to honor your spirit and not thinking everything you are told is true. Follow your own instincts as they probably are correct.

- Believe in loyalty. If my friend is insulted or hurt by another friend and she is innocent, it would be difficult for me to be friends with the person who insulted somebody I care about.

QUESTIONS FOR SELF REFLECTION

1. Have you ever trusted someone who turned out to lack integrity? Were you shocked to learn about that person?
2. Can you think of times you have behaved without any integrity?
3. Will you try to be more conscious of hurting other people if you are at fault?
4. Are you loyal to the people you most love and consider friends?

A person cannot be whole without integrity!

Notes

13

Dignity

How High Do You Hold Your Head?

T he word dignity is a beautiful word and dignified people are equally as beautiful. They act with grace and stand tall in spirit. Which celebrity stands out for you as a dignified person? I think Cary Grant as a man and Jacqueline Kennedy at the time her husband was assassinated. Dignity is self-respect. A dignified person holds their head high through thick and thin and handles situations without cursing, screaming or asking, "Why me?"

One of the most dignified people I know has been in a wheelchair since her late 20's. She was married with children living in the suburbs. She had a passion for horses and one day while riding she was thrown from her horse. Her horse fell on top of her, crushing her legs and confining her to her wheelchair for life. However, this didn't stop her from living a full life. She remains outstandingly beautiful; she's a renowned sculptor; a younger man fell deeply in love with her, and they have been together ever since. Riding in her handicapped cart, she takes herself out daily on errands. She fills a room with beauty and grace and her deep passion for horses remains. She never complains and has kept her incredible disposition.

My grandmother lost two daughters and carried a disposition like no other. She handled her devastating losses with dignity keeping the outside world from her pain. My daughter handled her five miscarriages with untold dignity. My sister handled the passing of her husband with great dignity by keeping him at home, converting her living room into a hospital room and taking care of him at every moment until he passed.

Dignity comes in all sizes and shapes. Being soft-spoken and noble are important to dignity.

One friend who has been diagnosed with cancer gets different answers from doctors. One says the cancer is all gone, then a few weeks later she is told, "It's back." She has been on this horrific seesaw ride for two years, trying to carry on living by having good times as she waits for the next diagnosis in her bizarre case. She manages to keep a high spirit, not allowing her friends to feel down in her company.

QUESTIONS FOR SELF REFLECTION

1. How do you define a dignified person?
2. Have you shown dignity during a traumatic time in your life?
3. If you were unable to handle your situation in a dignified manner, do you recognize your behavior? Have you learned from your past behavior?

Treating other people with dignity means we are treating them the way we would like to be treated ourselves!

Notes

14

Honesty

Held Up a Bank Yet?

Honesty is wonderful, telling the truth is powerful, and becoming an open person not only heals yourself but the people around you. Honesty is being sincere, truthful, trustworthy, honorable, fair, genuine, and loyal. Complete honesty is refreshing. Tell people your age—it's freeing. My grandmother never told anyone her age. We guess she was about ninety-five when she passed, but wouldn't it have been nice for us to know?

We appreciate people who do not bullshit us and know how to tell us the truth without stabbing us from behind. Telling a friend that they put on weight or that their new hairstyle looks terrible, can hurt their feelings more than you might realize. We can learn from and give constructive criticism if we use tact. Speaking in private is a necessity if there is something you want to say to someone that is not flattering.

Often we are afraid to admit a fault of ours to others. However, when we do, we gain respect. The other night when

I was performing a song, I forgot the words and apologized on the stage. That brought me more applause than if I had sung the song through perfectly. There are times we lie even to ourselves. When I was a kid I lied to my diary, elaborating and twisting the truth especially if it was about a boy who did not like me. How could I admit such a thing even to me? Can you imagine lying about your own self to your own self? What is gained or lost when you do this?

Then there are those that love to exaggerate and elaborate. For instance, they will tell you something cost $3000.00 when it really was $30.00; fifty people came, when there were only five. With this type of person we need to cut everything in half. They might feel more important by telling you something is bigger, more, better than it is.

This was voted the *"Best Answer, chosen by Asker, internet"* why people might exaggerate. They are simply lacking the attention whether emotionally or physically. They might feel they sound more interesting.

Children learn to lie when their parents put fear into them, and that lie becomes another lie. My son played hooky, thinking I was gone for the day. Instead there he was in the backyard with other hooky players, when I surprised him by coming home early. Will I ever forget the look on his face? I had to laugh to myself while I was forced to reprimand him ending his fun and exciting day. My daughter stole from a five and ten and got caught when she was about twelve years old. They called me in to the store, there she was in the managers office horrified. I cannot imagine a more honest person than my daughter as she grew up. From that embarrassing experience I believe she never wanted to do anything that might set somebody off. What about the person who may find money going to every extent to return it to you? Or the dishonest person who puts it in his pocket and never looks back. I have lost my wallet twice this year. Miraculously, I received an immediate call from the subway station manager that it had been found completely in tact. The next time, it came back to me through the post office, with everything intact except the cash; they had dropped it into a mailbox. I was thrilled both times to receive it back but had already gone through the trouble to replace my cards with the second loss. What took so long, I wanted to say.

Can you be honest with your own self?

Can you not put the blame on another person realizing that maybe it was you that caused the problem. Hmmmmm?

It is much easier to say, " If not for, or he said, and that is why." Stand up for yourself in every way including your faults.

There are some who are good at twisting the truth. They prefer not to tell the story straight so they twist things to confuse the person. They live by, "If you can't convince them, confuse them."

Then there is the man woman relationship. The woman asks,

"Please just tell me you had an affair. Just admit it and I will forgive you; I just want to hear the truth from you."The man admits to the affair and then she breaks up with him anyway. Who is being dishonest now?

SOME RECOMMENDATIONS FOR YOU

- Never let anyone take the blame for some dishonest act you were involved in.
- Don't deny your wrong doings; admit them fast.
- Being blatantly honest by causing pain in another person is not necessary.
- Return that found wallet ASAP.

QUESTIONS FOR SELF-REFLECTION

1. What category do you fall into? An honest person, an exaggerator, a little crooked? Would you keep the money and drop the rest of the wallet in the mailbox? How about calling the person yourself? Wouldn't that make you feel great?
2. If you have done some naughty stuff, how did it make you feel? Where you glad you were clever enough to get away with stuff or a bit remorseful?
3. If you fall into being an exaggerator or an elaborator can you define why you do it?
4. Have you told the truth to a friend when you saw their mate out with another person? Did it cause harm? Did the couple eventually get back to each together? When they did how did they react to you?

Let us honor the person who knows when to speak and even more so, the one who knows when to hold their tongue!

Notes

Now you are almost perfect.

Here comes amazing you!

15

Humble - encouraging - respectful - patient - kind

If You Possess All Of These Attributes, Hats Off To You!

An old Cherokee told his grandson, "My son, there is a battle between two wolves inside us all. One is Evil. It is anger, jealousy, greed, resentment, inferiority, lies & ego. The other is Good. It is joy, peace, love, hope, humility, kindness, empathy, & truth." The boy thought about it, and asked, "Grandfather, which wolf wins?" The old man quietly replied, "The one you feed."

The person who has fed themselves the sweets of life and has achieved being a joyous, peaceful, loving, humble, person who is kind, who has empathy and tells the truth, is one of God's little miracles.

When a person is **humble** it humbles me. Those who achieve great recognition and reach impressive goals, yet never boast or praise themselves blow my mind for their modesty. For me, achieving something that deserves recognition makes me scream out loud with joy and excitement, telling everyone I know. Some never speak of their accomplishments and we find out about them by reading an article or hearing where they were the night before. What makes this humble person tick? A humble person does not seem to consider themselves first. While they may possess superior intelligence they would not think of insulting or putting another person down for their lack of knowledge. Humble people either acquired the trait as they lived their life or had such an upbringing where they were taught to consider others before themselves. It is a lovely trait to possess.

Then there are those who **encourage** other people to follow their star even when others tell them to forget it. They care more about others and take the time to go deeper into another's dream and instill confidence. They make an effort to compliment others, to make them feel good and greet them with a smile. Nothing is more rewarding than a teacher who encourages a student to achieve goals. If it was not for my writing teacher and her easy-going attitude that kept encouraging me, I would not have become a writer. We all need encouragement in our lives and especially when we are learning something new or have a new idea. Here is to the person who can look you in the eye and say, "Keep going," it can make all the difference. I once took Spanish lessons and was asked to go to the board and write some words. I couldn't do it properly and my teacher said, " Sit down, you should have known that by now." I was humiliated and never went back to class. Teachers are there to encourage, Because I felt language would be a difficult thing for me to achieve, I decided to put my energy into other things.

What about that wonderful virtue called **patience**! If we are patient, most desires will be fulfilled. There is abundance on this planet and enough for everyone as long as we live healthy lives and are here to receive the goodness we all deserve. Patience like anything else has to be learned and takes discipline. We have to put aside our desire for the need to be first, push ahead of others or skip quickly to the end of your project. Most of all, love takes patience to develop. Perhaps more patience than anything else. Knowing another person takes years and even then, we may walk away scratching our heads. There is enough time with patience for everything to come our way. Patient people know that.

Then there are the people that treat others with **respect** only because they are a fellow human being. They do not say an unkind word about anybody. They give other people credit rather than taking it for themselves or robbing another of their ideas. They truly love people of all races, creeds, rich or poor; there are no dividing lines because they cannot see one. To respect someone means to admire their position in life, perhaps our elders, mothers, fathers, grandmothers, doctors, teachers. Couples who bicker in front of their children, who do not respect one another or support one another, can cause a lifetime of confusion and heartache to their child. The child is left without knowing what is right or wrong.

If you do not respect yourself it is almost impossible to respect others. Dressing poorly, unkempt, shows no respect for yourself.

My grandmother's most important word was "Respect." She placed herself high on the totem pole and lived her life as a respected person. She would teach me to live my life to be respected (especially when I began dating boys) Be a respectful neighbor. They live there too and are trapped with your disrespectful habits. Banging your door or playing your music loud so they can hear it or doing anything that might interrupt their quiet enjoyment is disrespectful. People frown upon a free spirit. If you are not one yourself, you will find nothing amusing about a free spirit; but they too must follow the rules of society.

Lastly, be **nice** and kind and try not to take things personally if someone is out of order.

The topics suggested in Part One are thoughts and ideas for you to explore while living a bigger better, happier, healthier, sexier and more vibrant exciting life style.

Now lets explore YOU some more!

Notes

Part 2

Your Health and Your Beauty

16

Doctors

Have They Become Your New Social Life?

P eople do get sick no matter how famous or extraordinary they might be. *We get old, things go wrong, but does that mean we have to act old?* May I ask, assuming you are in good health, how often do you visit your doctor? Some women talk more about their doctors than the reason for making an appointment. Overheard was this conversation between friends:

"My doctor is the best there is; there is no other like him; you **must** use him, he is the best in the field, trust me."

"No, I would not trade my doctor. He is caring, brilliant. I adore my doctor, I have complete faith and trust in him and wouldn't think of changing."

"If I was 10 years younger I would have an affair with my doctor."

(Come to think about it, I remember falling in love with my obstetrician at age twenty-two when I was pregnant with my first baby.)

Have you noticed that going to the doctors seems to be a growing social life pastime amongst seniors? It is all we hear about. It is all people seem to talk about. Waiting rooms are packed with doctors rarely running on schedule. Women take time dressing up for their appointments, forgetting they will be stripping down and changing into gowns without a glimpse from their hero.

Over the years learning to think more for myself, carefully evaluating doctors' orders, acting as my own doctor as well has proved to be worthwhile. Not to say their advice is not mostly correct, but taking time to evaluate what they said makes me feel more in control of me. While doctors are a blessing when we need them and we do all need them, it's important to remember that they are people too and can be wrong. Listen and evaluate their findings and opinions and if you are not convinced, seek other opinions. Nobody knows ourselves better than we do! For example, After going for a routine stress and heart test that proved to be perfect, the doctor wanted to see me again in three weeks. I asked,

"Why? You have just given me a good report, why must I come back so soon?"

She was taken aback. "Well, it is precautionary."

"That might be true, but even when you have a healthy report?"

When surgery was necessary a few years ago, I sought five opinions making sure of the procedure and the doctor. Scheduling my surgery with a clear head and feeling comfortable with my choice made it easier to go through the ordeal. While admitting five opinions may have been a bit over the top, three opinions, when it comes to something major, is advisable. Long ago not taking a doctor's word as gospel proved to be lucky for me. The OB-GYN who delivered my son recommended a hysterectomy after some minor symptoms. Since he was my doctor who I trusted there was no doubt about my going through with it until my friend said,

"Don't do it, wait and see if your problem clears up on its own."

The problem did clear up, with the minor symptoms never appearing again. If not for my friend, my body would have gone through an unnecessary ordeal with possible complications.

Think of the consequences when a medication is prescribed. What is the downside to that medication? Will there be side effects? Is it absolutely necessary or is there another way to cure the problem? Doctors know how to prescribe. Patients line their stomachs with pills and some find out that the effects are even worse than the symptoms. The point is, check for yourself, make sure for yourself; doctors are people too.

As human beings, we all want to be kind and helpful to a friend in need but listening and surrounding ourselves with the illnesses of others and their complaints will infringe on your own healthy living. In a retirement village, the conversations are even more contagious. Seeing and hearing about friends' and neighbors' traumas on a daily basis is difficult to avoid. There's always someone who has a problem. If you have been blessed with good health, try to stay clear of conversations about sickness. Dwelling or talking about your aches and pains brings negativity into your life. Talking about being old will make you feel old. Nature ages us; how you age and your attitude toward it depends completely upon yourself and the everyday care you give your body, mind and spirit. If you think young and vibrant chances are you will be. Do what is necessary to maintain your health by having your yearly checkups, eating well, exercising, and taking precautions. **Don't let an old person into your still-vibrant body no matter how old you are.**

We all know that stress is one of the worst things we do to ourselves. My blood pressure once hit 193 during a two-hour conversation with a Dell computer expert in India. He exasperated me by keeping me on the phone for almost two hours, but my reaction to him was much worse; threatening my own health. We place ourselves in danger when we are frustrated, angry, or hurt, allowing ourselves to cause terrible stress to our bodies, which could ultimately cause a stroke or a heart attack. Not having self control is immature, thoughtless behavior to yourself and others around you.

The good news is that there are more centenarians than ever before. In Japan alone there are 50,000 people over one hundred years old. In Australia, the Queen once sent birthday cards to anyone who reached one hundred years old. Eventually, she found her kind gesture was getting out of hand. One person has been reported to have lived to 115, another to 130. Now eighty-year-olds are running marathons and weight lifting.

Here is what the oldest man in the United States, Walter Breuning, has to say about the secret to long life: Embrace change, even when the change slaps you in the face." Every change is good." Eat two meals a day. "That's all you need." Work as long as you can. "That money's going to come in handy." Help others. "The more you do for others, the better shape you're in." Then there's the hardest part. It's a lesson Breuning said he learned from his grandfather: Accept death. "We're going to die. Some people are scared of dying. Never be afraid to die. Because you're born to die," he said.

With that said, for me it is about falling and breaking bones. Falling six times, breaking my bones three out of six has led me to many orthopedic doctors rehabs and scary uncomfortable down times.

FALLING:

My first fall was in my apartment at age 52, slipping and falling on a plastic bag on my hard wood floor, breaking my shoulder. One problem led to another, thinking healing would never happen. Miraculously, our body heals with time and much patience.

Then in East Berlin, the doors quickly shut while trying to pull my bag onto the train, throwing me onto the platform landing on my back. When you cannot get up, you know you are hurt, as it is our natural instinct. People gathered around as the sirens came towards me, reminding me of the same sirens as in *The Diary of Anne Frank*. Taken to a hospital ward in East Berlin filled with German women turned out to be amusing and giving all of us more laughs than if my travels had gone on. They released me after two weeks and I hobbled home to the U.S.

Next came falling off of a bike and breaking my wrist. It seemed old hat to me at this point; just another brace.

Then in China, while enjoying a lovely afternoon, sipping tea at a fine hotel, relaxing with a book in their elegant tea room, I stood up, took a look around the room, and missed the two steps down landing on the marble floor of the Ritz. Crowds surrounded me; the waiters gathered looking down on me in horror and shrieking all at once in Chinese. The worst so far was when I sublet my apartment for several months. Noticing a dirty spot on the floor of my apartment as I was leaving, I ran for the Clorox. The phone rang and forgetting that the floor was wet with slippery Clorox, my feet went out from under me, falling backwards and luckily landing on my elbow rather than my head. This one called for two elbow operations and on top of everything homeless making my three month healing process extremely challenging.

Then after a morning breakfast date with a boyfriend elated

and feeling happy from seeing him, I tripped on an uneven piece of sidewalk only a block from home. The ambulance came, the crowds formed; another broken wrist. Worse than the broken wrist, he never visited me or called for one month.

Falling incapacitates us; we go from vibrancy to dependency in a split second. Dressing, walking, sleeping, bathing, cooking are difficult if not impossible.

They start to happen when we are kids. Back then, we had scrapes and tears, but now it is about bones. Carole Channing once said that she has had so many broken bones, she stopped counting.

My lessons have been to slow down and to look down when walking, lifting my feet and reminding myself not to keep doing the scenario.

If you are prone to falling it is best to make sure your home is clear of obstructions, make sure rugs lie flat, be aware of water on the floor, and watch out for that slippery Clorox. There are training courses on how to prevent falls which are usually given at a senior community centers.

The minute my elbow healed, three months later, I left on a book signing tour for the next two months, driving myself from state to state and city to city. My elbow trauma was over, never looking back or having any fears about moving forward.

SOME RECOMMENDATIONS FOR YOU:

- Be careful!
- Don't overdo it with doctors appointments and medications. Is that upcoming doctor's appointment necessary? Is it a regular checkup or an appointment your doctor ordered even though you are fine?
- Check your medications with your doctor and make

sure what you are taking is still necessary. Perhaps question your doctor why it should be continued.

- The more medications you take, the easier it is to mix them up. Make sure you know and understand all of your pills or better still...... **Trade in your pills for passion.**
- Many hospital visits are caused by taking the wrong pill.
- Stop taking inventory of your aches and pains or talking about them.
- Only your closest of kin want to hear descriptions about your operation or health. The rest of us have our closest of kin to listen to.
- Exercise to improve your mood and health. Sitting, saddening and medicating because we have reached a certain age does not have to be your lifestyle.

QUESTIONS FOR PERSONAL REFLECTION

1. How often do you see your doctor for checkups?
2. Do you find yourself involved in conversations on an ongoing basis about health and what is happening to other people?
3. Do you talk about illnesses?
4. Do you think that getting older means illness and this is simply to be expected?

An apple a day will keep the doctor away as long as it is included with healthy eating, exercise and attitude.

Notes

17

Sleep

But Not Through it All!

It has been said, "If people had the right amount of rest, there would be no conflicts." Can you imagine how sleep deprived Bin Laden must have been, lying in bed at night, masterminding his horrors? I have often wondered how our Presidents function with their intense agendas of flying from country to country, arriving jet-lagged and then there are the businesspeople from around the world setting their alarms for an early morning meeting arriving from abroad. What is worse than the day after New Year's Eve waking up from a night of drinking and partying, groggy, head aching, out of sorts? We must sleep and sleep well.

Insomnia, which everyone experiences from time to time, can drive a person crazy! When it hits we try everything imaginable: sleeping pills, counting sheep, hot milk; we watch the hours go by, begging for sleep to come and sometimes it can take several days to overcome. Jet lag throws us off for days. We try pills, eating at a different time, going to sleep earlier/later before and after we fly. When flying from the East Coast to Europe, invariably jet lag comes over me at 1:00 P. M. begging for an afternoon of sleep.

Teenagers can sleep till 2:00 in the afternoon. A babysitter for my children slept so soundly it was as if she were deaf. Telephoning home to check on the kids during a movie night out, there was no answer. My husband and I ran from the theater imagining the worst; fire, break in, what could have happened in so short a time? Fear! Fear! Everything seemed calm enough as we pounded on our sitter's door, stamped our feet, called her name; but nothing would wake Voncille. She never heard the phone and that was the last of her. Many years later she married a friend of mine and I am sure she made a great mom.

Some people can fall asleep the minute they sit down in a comfortable chair, sleeping through anything. Some are already asleep before they hit the bed, hoping not to hit the floor. Others can be awakened by the slightest sound. A friend of mine stays up half the night and sleeps all day preferring her night life to her daytime activities. As we grow older we need less sleep. Some of us get away with four to five hours; but the majority of people need seven to eight hours. Sleeping well puts life on target, our minds are clear, unstressed, all is well, feeling we can whizz through a day of accomplishments. Sleep keeps us in better spirits and helps us enjoy a good day. Love your bed; It provides delicious nourishment for your soul and mind.

Resting and napping are equally important for health. One of my favorite things to do when tired, but yet not ready to sleep, is to lie in the dark, in bed, with no sound around me and deeply relax. My parents were in the retailing business and worked hard in their dress shop. They cleverly kept a bed in their back office, taking turns napping to get them through the long hours of retail. Naps are healthy. A friend of mine wished her seventy-plus mom wouldn't take naps, thinking she should be more active.

Her mom knew better; taking a nap rejuvenated her so she could lead a more active life. My daughter went to a spiritual retreat in New Mexico. During the first floor exercise, she looked around to see half of the room asleep. People are longing for rest. On the first days of a vacation, you will notice people fast asleep at the pool or the beach. In a small Greek village in the mountains of Crete, going to sleep at 7:00 PM or when the sun set, and awakening at 5:30 AM to a sky filled with stars, the air crisp and chilled was memorable. God created us to awaken at sunrise and go to sleep at sunset. Man has destroyed this natural order by filling ourselves with the exciting temptations of the night which is usually television.

Couples fight and break up over snoring or sleep habits. Homes are now being built with two master suites, recognizing that couples may want their own privacy. It makes sense: we had sleep patterns before we met our partners. Then suddenly there is another person lying next to us who came with their own sleep patterns, tossing, turning, snoring, coughing, talking. While it is a nice feeling to sleep next to the one we love, it is better to get a good night's rest. Years ago couples slept in single beds; remember Ozzie and Harriet? Then manufacturers started making our beds bigger and rounder and king sized.

One of our worst sounds is that of the alarm clock. There is little choice when we must be at a job or at school, but if we programmed our bodies properly we could forego the unwelcome sound of the alarm. We have our own ingrained time clock as invariably before the clock goes off I am already awakened. There is a new online wake up call which is quite amusing. After registering my cell phone number they call to test the line. Sure enough, Captain Wakeup called:

"This is Captain Wakeup," he says. "If you are awake press one."

SOME RECOMMENDATIONS FOR YOU:

- Prioritize sleep over watching a television program or a movie. A television program is not worth losing sleep over. Try not to get involved in a late night movie that starts at an appropriate time and ends way after.
- For people who have occasional insomnia or who simply can't fall asleep one night, try a pill from the health food store called Calms or another brand, which is mild and non-addictive.
- Get up, read, walk, watch TV, write, but don't go to the refrigerator.
- Stay off your computer as it could prove to be too stimulating, especially if you are researching.
- To help me fall asleep at night, I might lie on my pillow recalling the activities of the day focusing on other things than sleep.
- Change your sleeping position; move to the bottom of your bed, change the room temperature; turn on a small fan, put on an extra blanket or take one off.
- Set regular bed times.
- Try going to bed one hour later or earlier than accustomed if you tend to wake up after a few hours.
- If your spouse has bad sleeping habits, move to another space.
- Take a hot bath and drink a glass of warm milk in the tub before bed.
- Meditate, do yoga or any other exercise before going to bed.
- Use a sleep mask to block out any light and ear plugs to block out any sound.
- Put a radio or earphones on static; the constant static is a great sleep inducer.
- Teach your children or grandchildren to stick to their bed times so they can develop good sleep patterns.
- Invest in dark blackout shades so no light enters your room.

QUESTIONS FOR PERSONAL REFLECTION

1. Are you a good sleeper? Do you keep regular bed times?
2. If your partner's habits stand in the way of a good nights sleep, would you consider sleeping alone in another space?
3. Will you give up that late night television program for better nights rest?
4. If all else fails, will you see a sleep therapist?

There is nothing in the marriage vow that says, "Thou must sleep together." Give yourself good sleeping space.

Notes

18

Hygiene

Who Doesn't Love a Sweet-Smelling Person?

The question might be brash, but have you checked how you smell before you leave your home? I wonder why people do not check themselves or take pride in good hygiene. Perspiration is a nauseating smell to others, especially coming from under one's arm pits. Sweaty people think nothing of food shopping or eating in a restaurant after a tennis game or a long jog. Once on a bus, I sat next to a unkempt man who deliberately lifted his arm pits, knowing tourists were offended by his smell, sat back laughing as we all covered our noses and begged to get off of the bus. There are people who have constant perspiration problems; a girlfriend of mine no matter how well showered would sweat and have a constant smell. Then there are those who become nervous or stimulated and begin to perspire and smell as the evening goes on even though they started out fresh. Sometimes nervousness can cause perspiration.

Not only does our skin have to be clean to avoid odor; our clothes have to be clean. A woolen sweater worn repeatedly without washing begins to smell from underarm perspiration. Wool should not be worn next to the body, especially if you are out for a long day where the temperature could climb. Wool especially tends to hold in perspiration, so wear a short cotton tee or such underneath. Changing your underwear is a daily must.

It is better to wash clothes rather than having them dry cleaned. Most clothing can be washed with care even though the label says something different. I wash practically everything right down to "down" quilts. If you are going to dry clean, use an organic cleaner so harsh chemicals will not touch your skin.

Some shoes such as workout shoes hold perspiration especially if you are not wearing socks. Talcum powder and shoe sprays help, and so does a washing machine. Once on a plane a man next to me kicked off his sandals, filling my seat with his horrendous foot smells. I breathed in the odor until I could not restrain myself any longer. With a soft voice, I asked,

"Won't you please put your shoes back on?" At first he was taken aback but then he did oblige me. I thanked him graciously and in the end we both smiled at each other.

Another problem area for odors is our hair. Know your hair and how often it needs to be washed. Hair that has not been washed looks oily, greasy and dirty and others can readily smell the grease.

What about bad breath? I thought blowing into hands was a good breath test but have recently learned differently. A sure test is to put saliva on your inner wrist as you would perfume and smell. For me speaking or eating until my teeth are brushed is a no no. Change your toothbrush often, floss, water pick, spray, test, what ever it takes to keep your breath fresh and clean. Garlic, of course, causes bad breath and some people retain the odor more than others. Here again, if you had garlic the night before, take extra precaution in the morning realizing that you might still smell. When you eat pure and fresh foods, you will notice a difference in your stool and your breath in a more positive way. Believe it or not my dinner dishes are cleaner when I load them into the dishwasher after a vegetarian meal. In addition, it is suggested to have your teeth cleaned three times per year.

Sometimes women's hormones change and while we might not have had facial hairs at one time, we now might see whiskers growing. When I was in my fifties I was unaware of the hairs growing around my chin and someone had to tell me. I was horrified now, always paying attention to any unwanted hairs. Some men grow hairs out of their nose and don't realize they are there. The new threading process that is springing up all over is terrific and unlike those painful electrolysis sessions. It is fast and clean with some bearable pain and it works.

Hygiene is important not just to make other people comfortable around us, but for everyone's health. Look at the cruise industry and how illness is passed from one guest to another. The cruise industry is aware and has hand sanitizer all over their ships. They also ask you to sign an affidavit stating that you are not boarding the boat sick; although I wonder how many people sign, even when they not they are feeling well. We no longer allow food to be eaten at our Mah Jongg games as the pretzels, cheese, fruit, nuts etc. were getting on to our hands, then the tiles.

Many times I have borrowed a phone and smelled the owner's scent on the phone; it is also an easy way to catch germs. Germs also can easily be transposed through using a microphone and one woman brought her own mic, messing up the sound system. Thin rubber gloves, while once a doctor's item, are now used for almost anything and time.

Shaking hands unfortunately is a custom that carries germs. It's impossible to think where a person's hands were before they touched yours. Have you been in a position while dining in a restaurant when a person approaches your table with a handshake? How do we not insult someone by not shaking their hand? I prefer the Asian way of putting our hands together in a prayer position and saying, "Namaste." If you do plan to shake hands, carry a hand sanitizer or go wash them straight away. This is how most of us end up getting sick.

Do you cover up your non-showered body with perfume? Much has been said about perfume and how offensive your perfume scent might be to other people. You and your mate might like how your smell, but the person stuck in line at the bank might find your perfume offensive. Strong perfume leaves a trail wherever it goes. If you do use perfume, try to use little to satisfy your final finishing touch. On the contrary, many times I have run after a woman to ask her what scent she is wearing. Some of the flowering scents that are natural to me are divine when it is kept light.

Men for the most part love women's vaginal smells. How true it is I am not sure but a doctor once gratefully told me that our odors do not seep out. Unlike bad breath or perspiration others can not smell what is going on in our private parts, such as an infection or other problems.

There's a lot more to table hygiene and manners than picking up the correct fork. Using your napkin to blow your nose at the table when you are eating is offensive. Always be aware of food on your mouth, and avoid slurping, chewing with your mouth open or *digging* your fork and knife into your plate to cut shows a stressed out person. One of my most embarrassing moments in table manners came when I was in my twenties and out for lunch with a friend. She ordered a fruit salad that looked great, so without asking I leaned over and dug my fork into her bowl helping myself to a piece of her fruit. She looked at me and said,

"Take the whole thing."

It is extremely embarrassing to tell someone that they smell and there has never been an easy way around this. The question is: Shall I grin and bear it or be rude or insulting and tell the person as I did on the plane? My sister and I have a pact to tell each other if we are offensive in any way. The foods that we eat, the diet we follow have has much to do with how our breath and body smells.

There is nothing as lovely as a sweet smelling woman or man. A man who I travelled with did not use the toilet in our room as he thought the odor even with a spray might offend me. He went down the hall to use the common bathroom. I was blown away by his brilliant etiquette.

SOME RECOMMENDATIONS FOR YOU:

- Shower or bathe each day and be sure to pay special attention to your underarms. Use a natural toothpaste like Tom's and a small wire pick that goes between the teeth.

- Before boarding a plane make sure you are showered and wearing deodorant. This is close quarters and for many hours. Be considerate by not being unkempt.

- Apply an organic deodorant that is good for your skin and read labels when it comes to applying anything on to your skin. Look for natural ingredients and avoid products with ingredients that you do not recognize. They will be chemicals rather than natural ingredients.

- You cannot wash your hands too often. If you do shake hands, carry a hand sanitizer.

- Baths are delightful but do not remain in the bathtub for long periods of time as the hot water is drying to skin. Bathing by candlelight or dim lights is soothing.

- Placing your handbags on tabletops means putting germs where you eat and prepare food. This is something we do not readily realize and a sure way to carry lots of unwanted germs home with us.

QUESTIONS FOR PERSONAL REFLECTION

1. Are you aware of your daily hygiene?
2. Have other people offended you by their odors?
3. Do you consider other peoples reaction to your perfume? The fragrance that you love can ruin somebody's day if you are in their presence.

Wash your hands often. It is the best way to keep yourself germ free!

Notes

19

Manicure and Pedicure

Now For Men and Children Of All Ages; Have You Noticed?

Ladies and gentlemen, please make sure the skin under your nails is clean. Is having a professional manicure and pedicure second nature to you or are you capable of grooming your own nails and toes? Many women simply do not like having a professional manicure/pedicure and enjoy taking care of their own. There are women who take greater pride in taking care of their finger nails than other parts of their body.

Years ago, a manicure and pedicure were very costly and manicurists were few and far between. Then the Asian people got smart by coming to America and opening salons. They were experts at it, the cost was minimal and people began to flock. The first time that I went to a Korean nail salon was in

New York City on 72nd Street in 1985. It was called Agnes nails and it was up the stairs on the second floor and cost five dollars compared to the fifteen I had been paying and she was excellent. Agnes nails has turned over many times until an older Korean couple bought the salon. They struggle hard to keep it going as now there are at least twelve salons within a few block radius and competition is enormous. The Koreans work long hours; having your nails done is possible seven days a week at practically any hour. Spa manicures with chairs that massage my body and neck at the same time my feet are being primped are delicious. In my neighborhood, a spa pedicure is offered where they massage my feet and legs for one hour. Ahh!

I will never forget my mom. She sat tall at a dressing table applying nail polish and refusing to go to her doctor's appointment until her nails were done. I noticed a little girl about two and a half years old sitting quietly staring at the manicurist as she polished her toe nails as if it already was second nature. I took my granddaughter for a manicure when she was ten thinking it would be a rare treat. I was surprised to see how properly she sat in the chair realizing then that she had sat that way many times before.

I once offered a gentlemen friend of mine a pedicure and manicure and he was insulted. What is wrong with my toes and nails? Plenty I wanted to say. Men are still much in the minority when it comes to manicures but lately more and more are having it done and it is great to see. Men do not realize how much a woman appreciates a well groomed man who sports clean nails and especially evenly cut toe nails.

Nowadays a simple manicure might not be enough. There are many beautiful designs to chose. This was a tweet I read: "There are cool fingernail polish designs, crazy nail polish designs, geeky nail polish, nerdy nail polish, ninja turtles, wacky nail polish, intense nail polish, nail art, nail designs, nail polish for 50-year-olds, Simpsons nail polish, twitter nail polish, there are nails with painted fruit, sports figures, photographs, polka dot nails and each nail or two a different color." You might enjoy Googling nail designs and viewing this new art.

My personal favorite shades are soft silver and I greatly favor the metallic shades. I also love the same white they use for a French manicure on my entire nail. However, what is more glamorous than long, bright red nails? Years ago there was red and orange period; now every imaginable color from green to blue to yellow to purple are in style. Many times I use a clear polish so that I do not have to worry about chipped polish.

There are literally hundreds of products on the market to smooth away dry skin such as organic products sold in health food stores. For over the counter, I like Jason brand products and the popular Burt's Bees is good. There are lime and ginger salt glows that can rejuvenate your hands and then nourished and conditioned with a good moisturizer. Soaking your feet in aromatherapy oils feel delicious.

SOME RECOMMENDATIONS FOR YOU

- I have found nothing that beats olive oil or Vaseline for dry skin. Rub it into hands and feet and cover with a white sock while you sleep. Voila!
- A good manicurist will not cut your cuticles. Cut cuticles grow back even more jagged.
- Using a razor that removes callouses is not a good idea as they grow back harder. Use a strong rough buffer instead.
- Rubber gloves are essential to wear when cleaning or working with your hands.

QUESTIONS FOR PERSONAL REFLECTION

1. Can you remember having your first manicure or have you still not treated yourself?
2. Are your nails an important feature or do you hardly pay attention to them, thinking who notices anyway?
3. Do you admire people with beautiful hands or look at women who have neatly polished toes?
4. Are you disgusted by those men and women who have dirty nails, especially if they sit down to dine with you?
5. Would you make a commitment to keep your hands soft and smooth and your nails lovely, paying as much attention to your nails as to other parts of your body?

Treat yourself to a day at the spa, massage, manicure and pedicure. You deserve it all. Oh yes, a facial too!

Notes

20

Hair

Oh No, Not Another Bad Hair Day!

How do you wear yours? Are you continually searching, changing, cutting, coloring, wigging, extending? Are you happy with your hairstyle or do you envy other women's hair? Have you tried to copy a beautiful celebrity's hairstyle thinking you will look like her? Why not? Try it, just be realistic. The trick is to "stay in style" and to let go of what did look well on you years ago. An old hairstyle will take away from your new amazing look.

Please don't tell me that you have cut your long hair because you no longer think it is age-appropriate? It broke my heart to see a friend cut her beautiful locks at age forty only because she did not feel her long flowing wavy blonde hair was age appropriate. As we age, longer hair reminds us of freedom and youth. What is that certain age," that your mind and spirit decided long hair was not the way you should look?

If you are blessed with long lovely hair, it should remain part of you always. Perhaps you will change the style by blowing it straight if it is curly, or curling it if it is straight. Maybe you will try to keep the ends a bit neater or pull the sides up. Cutting it short will be doing an injustice to yourself. If nature does not want you in long hair, you will either begin to go bald or your hair will disintegrate. That has been my decision on keeping my hair longer, nature will tell me when it is time. A hairdresser once told me that most women wear ponytails or pinned back hair for their day-to-day living. Are you a woman who has long hair but have resorted to only wearing an up do, then perhaps a short stylish haircut may be right for you. Otherwise hold on to your locks! Enjoy what you have grown. I don't think anyone likes to get a haircut if you favor hair long; even a trim can be stressful.

I enjoy so many hairstyles that it has been difficult for me to find just one. I love bangs, side parts, middle parts, curly hair, tight curls, loose curls, straight slinky hair, upsweeps and braids in pigtails and braids around the head. Because of this, incognito I go! I often wondered why new acquaintances have no recollection of who I am when they meet me the second time, finally realizing that my hair turns me into a chameleon. The very best way to find a good hairdresser is to admire someone's style and to ask that person who does her hair. I followed a woman into the ladies room; "I love your haircut, where did you have it done?" She was proud to tell me and I immediately made an appointment. Her hairdresser first told me that her texture was different and her cut would not work well on me. I asked him, What do you suggest? He stared at my hair, played with my hair tossing it up and around and back and forth and then said,

"Your hair cut is perfect, go home." Of course he has won my confidence so when the time comes, I will go to him.

Having attended an all-senior audience and sitting in the back of the audience, before me were rows and rows of gray-haired women with exactly the same hairstyle. The look was neat, trimmed, bobbed and teased hair with loads of hair spray. All of these women had longer, darker, blonder, redder hair at one time. They have put themselves into a box and each one looks like the other making their statement,

"My youth is gone; I am grey, so I will simply cut it short like every other grey haired friend of mine."

Perhaps some of these women should converse with their spouses to see what they think about the girl they married. There are many other choices a woman can make other than bobbed grey hair.

If your hair is turning gray, resist chopping it all off and then dipping your head into a vat of black dye. Hair that is obviously dyed is harsh. Do research or try on a wig for better insight. There is a website where you can actually insert your photo and get great ideas. "Dailymakeover.com." Nowadays hair colors are not harsh and home kits are affordable.

Back in my teens we would experiment on each other's hair and what a disaster that was. One friend acted as a mad chemist, mixing colors and guaranteeing that she knew what she was doing. Once I came out bright orange. It was once hard to find a salon with expertise on bleaching hair; most were not experts. It took me many long years, many tears, and many colorists to finally settle on my shade. Now I have my hair color down to a T and rather than take any chances I bring in my well-developed formula and have it applied correctly. Not every salon allows you to do that so if you like the idea, seek someone who is willing to apply the color of your choice. Be daring; you can be a blonde, a redhead, a brunette, highlighted and if you don't like that one you can change back. One woman bleached the top half of her dark hair and bangs in grey color. I will say it was different; almost like a permanent hat on her head. Women who have maintained their **thick** long hair that has turned grey is lovely. Then a greying woman should not color her hair, especially if it is silver grey. For the rest of us, when you begin to see grey hairs that are becoming wider at your scalp, it might be best to seek professional help at a salon to prepare for your first entrance into colored hair. Now is the time to be careful and not to choose just any salon or colorist. Your homework is to the find the right person at the right salon. Too many hairdressers simply do not know hair even though they can fool the best of us. It might be worth your while to spend money the first time by going to a top salon for a consultation. Some will tell you the right product and right color for your hair. You can then try to duplicate it at a salon that is not as expensive.

We women love the beauty parlor! Even in a recession there are still beauty parlors and they are filled. When you go to a salon and especially after you have taken the time to educate yourself as in above, please make sure you do not allow your hairdresser to take over and do what they want to do when it comes to anything permanent. Some may feel insulted, but it is your hair and it must be a mutual realistic agreement. After all, don't they want you to return? Most of us have at one time come home crying due to a bad haircut or bad color because of being convinced that the hairdresser knew what was best. I also remember wanting to change my hairdresser but was afraid to insult him/her and don't be fooled, some do get highly insulted. After listening to their side, don't be shy; speak up and tell them what you think is right for you. If you agree to a haircut and if length is important to you, let them show you their first snip to see how much they have taken off. It is best not to trust as at that moment they can be lost in thought and there goes your length. Fortunately, hairdressers are a little less pompous in recent years especially when it comes to a cut. Lie back, have your hair washed with a fine shampoo, have your scalp massaged. Enjoy the treat of going to the beauty parlor; let it become a necessity and rewarding time. There is no argument that color makes a woman look brighter, younger and prettier.

Some women simply do not want to be bothered with their hair especially in summer and cut it into an unflattering style. Boy cuts are terrific especially for those that dye it a fun color. Some short cuts can be glamorous and sexy. I love and admire hair; it is a woman's and man's jewel. I would rather look at the beautiful hair nature has given us, than a gorgeous piece of jewelry.

Then there are those women who look extremely youthful from behind. Then they turn around and we see that their hair does not fit their body. This is where we have to be careful. Try to do away with berets, bows and cute little ornaments, ribbons and bands or possibly an eloquent clip might enhance a formal hair style. We have to stay in tune with our mind, body, and spirit so that we look coordinated in stature from top to bottom and from back and front is essential.

Weather directly affects our hair. If you live in the tropics and have curly hair, it will usually become curlier, straight hair usually does not stay straight or may fall limp. Rainy weather effects hair and so does humidity. In our twenties a friend covered her hair when she went out in the sun; she knew then how to take care of her lovely hair. It took me way past that to learn not to venture out without a hat or putting my hair up and out of the way of weather. Hair is the crowning glory and no matter how expensive our clothes are, if our hair does not look good, somehow we don't look good.

Here is an article that supports my thinking. According to *T. Veto the Matronly Look*:

If you decide to keep your hair long and want to pull it up on top of your head, it doesn't have to be sprayed and stiff and look like a helmet, according to T. Veto BecomeGorgeous.com. You don't have to follow. The cardinal rule used to be, that when a woman turned 30, and certainly if she were a mother, that her long locks had to go. That was back in a more rigid era, however, when there was a rule for everything and women, in particular, tended to obey them. If you are 50 or beyond and want to wear your hair long or dye it purple, go ahead and do it. Wear the style you think is the most flattering to you and thumb your nose at ridiculous rules. (exactly my feelings) *You do not have to look matronly just because you're on the far side of 50.*

According to *Micheal Cheal and Angel Wheeler for SL Hairstyles*:

Note that if a woman has short, chunky layers around her face it will emphasize her eyes rather than her slack jawline. Because older women have to deal with the effects of aging, including dryer and thinner hair, Cheal and Wheeler also advise that short shags and layered crop tops work very well for hair that has seen better days. If you choose to wear your hair long, however, consider wearing it in an up-do, such as a French roll. Again, you are directing the eye upward and this will detract from the flaws that are occurring due to age. Lifting the hair up and keeping some height on top will make you look taller and leaner. Hair length is no longer dictated by society and age. Pick your hair style based on your facial structure, the type of hair you have and your lifestyle. According to an article written by Paul Jones for HairdoHairstyles.com, your choice of haircuts and styles is limited only by what fits you, your face, your complexion, your hair texture and, perhaps, primarily, your personality. Older women do, in fact, generally have thinner hair, due to post-menopausal hormone deficiencies, and possibly not as much hair as they did when they were younger. Do not despair. A short hairstyle may be best for disguising thin hair, because people may look at your face rather than your hair. Consider getting your hair cut into a bob and think about getting some bangs, which will cover up forehead wrinkles.

Layering hair around the face and brushing it slightly back and upward, rather than downward, is a great way to soften your facial features. Women tend to want to do the opposite and opt for styles that keep the hair close to their face, because they think this will disguise their loosening jaw line. Styling the hair with the front portion being slightly shorter around the face and then layered in back actually works better, according to Paul Jones for HairdoHairstyles.com. If you use a round brush, which will fluff up your hair, this will give your hair some lift and, once again, take attention away from those areas of your face that are aging. When the hair is moving upward it will counteract the downward slide of your facial features, which happens with age. If you have always preferred short hair, then that is who you are. But If you have cut it only because you are of a certain age, think otherwise. Don't feel that you must wear your hair short because you are older. It's a myth that unnecessarily robs some of us a feminine touch, and it does not make us look a day more youthful

QUESTIONS FOR PERSONAL REFLECTION

1. Do you have a really bad hair story? I imagine we all have one of those, but was there a particular time?
2. Are you still seeking your individual look and have never been altogether satisfied with your present look?
3. What hairstyle makes you feel the best? Are you holding onto a style you wore in high school?
4. Does weather affect your hair?
5. Are you able to be completely honest with your stylist? Watch that first snip closely.
6. Would you like to make a change, but are afraid of what your friends and family might think?
7. Would you spend money to get a hair makeover?
8. Sometimes, you'll feel better just by making a change in your hairstyle. No look lasts forever; so why not try a great new hairstyle?

Glory be! Your hair. If you have long locks, enjoy them forever.

Notes

21

Sun Damage

Who Put Those Brown Spots on My Lovely Skin?

I am damaged.

In my teens, twenties and thirties, lying on the beach from 8:30 am till 5:00 PM, getting tan, made me feel really good. Dark tan was the way to go and the darker the better! With my friends we tanned on rooftops, covering ourselves in baby oil and iodine while holding a sun visor to attract more sun. If we had only known! At age thirty-one I had perfect skin, by that I mean there was not a spot on my skin even though I had been tanning for fifteen years.

As we all *might* know it takes many years for our skin to show sun damage and now that gorgeous tan, forty years later, has left my arms and legs covered in dark brown ugly spots that are impossible to remove. Simply know that as you bask in the beautiful sunshine that we all love, you are forming in prints for dark spots to surface many years later. It took years for the

Skin Cancer Foundation to begin to educate us. Not all skin is effected in the same way but most of us must stay out of the sun or have the repercussions of blotchy skin, brown spots and/or skin cancer. For me and my spots, the only way out is to tattoo over them (just kidding readers). There are lasers but I have been told when you have any sun exposure they come right back. Maybe someday they will invent a machine where we can stand tall putting out our arms and legs and miraculously receive perfect new skin. One friend who is well spotted said,

"I need all new skin."

For me, it is too late as there are far too many spots to remove, but not for you. Apply sunscreen daily and stay out of direct sunlight. If you begin to see age spots that you have not seen before, visit your dermatologist and have them zapped. It is both painless and affordable. There are many products on the market that claim they can make your dark spots disappear but so far I cannot swear by one. Any dermatologist will advise you as to which one might work best for you.

A few years ago I began to use a sun bronzer from the tube and thought this was the way to go and not realizing that they were intensifying my spots.

"According to editor Valerie Monroe, in the July 2007, issue of O the Oprah Magazine," if you have hyper pigmentation (dark spots), you should avoid self-tanners, which tend to darken age spots. If you have hypo pigmentation or light age spots tanner will help even out your skin tone."

Besides sunspots there is, of course, the danger of skin cancer.

Since its inception in 1979, The Skin Cancer Foundation has always recommended using a sunscreen with an SPF 15 or higher as one important part of a complete sun protection regimen. Sunscreen alone is not enough, however. Read this full list of skin cancer prevention tips: Seek the shade, especially between 10 AM and 4 PM. Do not burn. Avoid tanning and UV tanning booths, Cover up with clothing, including a broad-brimmed hat and UV-blocking sunglasses, Use a broad spectrum (UVA/UVB) sunscreen with an SPF of 15 or higher every day. For extended outdoor activity, use a water-resistant, broad spectrum (UVA/UVB) sunscreen with an SPF of 30 or higher, Apply 1 ounce (2 tablespoons) of sunscreen to your entire body 30 minutes before going outside, Reapply every two hours or immediately after swimming or excessive sweating, Examine your skin head-to-toe every month, See your physician every year for a professional skin exam.

SOME RECOMMENDATIONS FOR YOU

- Always wear a hat when you go out in the sun; keep your hair covered in the hot sun.

- There are sun screen products for your hair as well.

- Always use sunblock, even in the winter time and rainy days too.

- If you live in sunny weather and drive, wear a long sleeve or long glove and a hat. Sunglasses are not enough.

- Try a tanning salon on a special occasion only.

- If you use a moisturizer with sunscreen in it, it is usually not enough protection.

- Use extra sunscreen on your chest, those freckled chests dark spotted chests are not becoming.

- LaRoche-Posay 45 is an excellent sun block found in drugstores.

- Many styling aids, leave in conditioners, and hair sprays have an SPF right in them! While I've heard varying options on how high the SPF should be for your hair, it seems that the consensus is to use an SPF of 10-15 in hair products, with SPF 12 being a very popular choice by many hair product manufacturers.

- If you are at a stage of life where you are just beginning to see sun spots have them zapped right away and I mean right away.

QUESTIONS FOR PERSONAL REFLECTION

1. Do you use sun screen when you leave your home?
2. Do you apply it to your children and grandchildren? This is important especially with children that surf or live in beach and ski areas.
3. Are you a sun worshipper that believes it is important to have vitamin D and do not worry about sun damage?
4. Has this writing helped to change your mind about taking precaution? We all know by now what is best, but do you practice it?

For goodness sake,
please stay out of the sun.

Notes

22

Makeup

Don't Leave Home Without It!

I am grateful for being a woman and seeing myself transformed on even the worst of days! Is there anything more fun than buying new makeup, especially for an occasion or having a makeup artist transform us for that special event? Does anybody remember the pancake makeup back in the fifties? My ex husband liked me without makeup and wondered how it could be possible, but maybe the thick pancake was not as flattering as it was thought to be. There are some who feel beautiful without makeup so decided to try an experiment by my not wearing makeup for a week. Nothing much happened good or bad, so went back to my preference. **MAKEUP!**

I have seen makeup cabinets so full that products pouring from the top shelf almost hit me in the face. Makeup drawers so full that I wondered how an eye shadow could be found. On the other hand, perhaps you are a woman who simply owns one tube of lipstick. Having my share of cosmetics, it feels good to minimize. I have it down to one of each; base color, concealer bronzer, eyebrow brush, eye liner, eye shadow, rouge and several shades of lipsticks. I like Mac liquid makeup base and their "Mac Red" lipstick is terrific. My eyes are green and deep purple shadow brings them out more than matching my eye color.

Is drugstore makeup any different than a leading brand? In drugstores we cannot open the product making it hard to judge how it will actually look at home and have been stuck many times. However, if you know what you like and if what you like looks good on you, there is little difference and you will be saving some money, although drugstore makeup has become expensive as well. Certain high end makeup companies' products were attacked this year for having inferior ingredients. It comes down to the special attention we might get from a speciality store or counter and sampling and a good way to test a new product. I have learned not to buy on the spot having the cosmetician write down what they used, going home and looking in my own mirror. If I like what I see, I go back and purchase. This is a wonderful idea to adapt for most purchases.

Moisturizing our skin is one of the most important things we can do before applying makeup. I like putting a drop of oil on my face after making up which takes away dryness. Invest in good brushes. A good brush will last for years if you take care of it or don't lose it; they make a positive difference in application. Recently eyebrows have come into focus. I have just received a gift of a special thin brush with a pointed edge to apply the shade of my eyebrows.

While mascara looks wonderful I have yet to find a brand that can be easily removed. Have you tried the new lengthening for eyelashes? One day I noticed a change in a friend's eyes. Suddenly her eyelashes grew making her eyes look beautiful. She had been applying a liquid on to her lashes making them grow. It is best to follow the rule that less is more. A beautiful woman is ageless.

SOME RECOMMENDATIONS FOR YOU

There are thousands of makeups and colors out there. Keep your face clean moisturized and sun screened and learn what looks good on you. Don't overdo it.

QUESTIONS FOR PERSONAL REFLECTION

1. Have you been wearing the same makeup or color for years?

2. Have you ever had a professional make you up? Would you like to have it done? Department stores will do it for free. There are also makeup schools where you can bring your own makeup and have a professional teach you to apply it with more expertise. Recently, I did exactly that while picking up a few good pointers. It was fun and learned a couple of little tricks such as putting concealer over my eyelids before applying shadow.

3. When you see a shade of lipstick that you like on someone else, do you ask her what color she is wearing so you can try it for yourself?

Wearing makeup makes a large difference so enjoy being the woman that you are by not leaving home without it!

Notes

23

Teeth

Old Yellow?

Teeth get old, just like our bodies. Amongst my circle of friends, only one person does not need dental cosmetics. She told me she brushed and flossed after each meal. Maybe there is something to it. Duh! Most of us are running to dentists, needing bridges, caps, implants, new bone, or dentures (like the ones that come out at night). People have receding gums, bleeding gums, loss of bone, and huge periodontal problems. It is not about cavities; it is about the aging of teeth and, worse than that, old discolored teeth.

I let my teeth go for a long time because to me they were not all that bad. They had served me well, didn't cause me any discomfort, and in this department I was not vain. Then, one day, I woke up and said,

"Those teeth no longer belong in my mouth."

After taking a good look in the mirror, I realized my gum line was receding, my teeth seemed shorter than I thought they were, suddenly my smile became something I preferred not to do, I have always been aware of other people's bad teeth, but mine? My sister had mentioned to me that my teeth needed fixing but I was not ready. My boyfriend told me how he takes care of his own teeth realizing later he was hinting for me to do something about mine.

When I was thirteen, I broke my front tooth when a boy tried to put his arm around me in the movies. I jerked forward and hit my tooth on the seat in front of me, coming back to his arms with a half of one tooth. I called the usher who came with a flashlight to look for the missing part of my tooth. I thought it could be glued back on. While I did not think it was that serious, it proved to be a great nuisance all of my life. My caps constantly broke or were not the same color.

Life is about smiles, and teeth are what people see when we smile. A smile makes us approachable-- the shortest distance between two people. A smile shows confidence, and if we are ashamed of our smiles, we deprive ourselves and others of a more positive world. Personally, I prefer to see wrinkles and sagging skin rather than bad teeth.

There are, for example, many teeth whiteners out there that will help brighten you up. After doing some research, Aquafresh seems to be a good teeth whitener. It is cheaper that Crest Whitestrips and seems to work better. Crest white strips are decent but expensive. If cost is important the cheaper drugstore brands are the best buy of all but must be used for two weeks instead of one, but can be used twice a day instead of once in order to cut out the second week. Whiteners must be used two to three times a year. Dentists as well will whiten your teeth at a much higher cost.

Since nature steps in around age sixty-five and arrives almost at the same time for all of us, it is best to head straight to the dentist because your teeth will not get any better. Most of us will eventually need cosmetic dental surgery--caps, bridges, implants--so pick a great, attractive doctor, or at least one who is entertaining, because you are going to be with him or her for a long time! Little did I know what an expensive ordeal it would be. It is not usually painful, but you can expect many visits for x-rays, molds, and fittings.

There are several ways to save money. Many dental schools will give you great discounts. Students do the work with an experienced doctor who oversees the procedure. This is a great way to cut costs if you have the time since it will most probably take longer than your own dentist to get finished. Another friend went on a dental vacation to Mexico where it is much cheaper, even with air, room, and board. This was in San Miguel, Mexico. She told me, "Two to three times a week, there I was at the dental office while in between, enjoying the beautiful sunshine and happiness of Mexico." People visiting India might stop in for some dental work where the dentists are excellent and a lot more affordable. There are many wonderful doctors out of the U.S. The only downside is if there are any repercussions it is usually a long trip back and it can be frustrating. One of my friends took a different approach by checking herself into the hospital. The doctor put her under, did all of the dirty work, and adhered her temporaries. When she woke up, she had a whole new set of teeth. In her case she was petrified of the dental chair and the dentist was more petrified of her sitting in his dental chair.

Most of us will be able to get caps or have posts put into the mouth to hold a new cap. For those who do not have bone enough to adhere, a removable bridge might be the answer. While one must try to keep their own teeth, but can not for various reasons, by all means get teeth that are removable. In the end it will not matter as the goal is to smile wide with beautiful white teeth. Make sure, once again, that you choose the right dentist who will take pride in making your teeth look natural. In the end the result will be the same as you will have beautiful white perfect teeth.

For my approach, I started with my top teeth, thinking, "Who cares about my bottom teeth? They hardly show." That was until the tops were done. I immediately followed through on the bottom teeth and suggest you do the same as the contrast will be evident. For me, it took about fifteen months to complete with lots of preparation and temporaries. I remember being horribly embarrassed as a temporary fell out of my mouth at a dinner party. To this day, I don't know if the person saw me try to catch it before it landed on my plate.

Hopefully, you have paid attention to your teeth. There is a wonderful product out there called bloodroot that is great for healthy gums, an extract to fight plaque and gingivitis. Dentists do not know much about this product, but bloodroot can be found in health stores. It is a miracle if you are having bleeding gum problems. Take every precaution in preserving your teeth and gums and maybe you will be one of the lucky ones. Keep your teeth strong and be careful how you chew. Avoid peach pits at all costs.

Listen to your dentist: brush, floss, water pick or thin brushes that fit between your teeth are advisable. Remember, the commercial brands of toothpaste contain sugar. Therefore, use only a natural toothpaste, such as Toms for one good brand.

QUESTIONS FOR PERSONAL REFLECTION

1. Have you noticed a change in your teeth or gum line?
2. Are your teeth discolored or uneven?
3. Do you notice other people who have bad teeth? Have you tried to whiten them with drugstore whiteners? Are the costs too prohibitive? If so, have you looked into your local dental school?

Take care of me all your life. I am your pearly whites.

Notes

24

Smile And Laughter

As Often As You Can And As Hard As You Can!

I n my final chapter under health and beauty I would like to include smile and laughter. While our faces can show many expressions, nothing is more pleasing than a smile. It can change your day and will ultimately change the day of others. Frowns do not look well nor do they make other people happy, but a smile lights up the world.

Robert Provine, Ph.D. (copied from internet May 21,12 has a wonderful way of looking at smiles. He feels, "The World Looks Beautiful While Smiling, Smile is a Symbol of Our Love to Others, Smiling Makes Us Attractive, Smiling Changes Our Mood, Smiling Is Transmittable Smiling Reduces Stress, Smiling Improves Your Immune System, Smiling Reduces Your Blood Pressure, Smiling is a Natural Drug, Smiling Makes You Beautiful and You Look Younger, Smiling Makes You Seem Successful, Smiling Helps Stay Positive, Smiling is linked with Heart and Wisdom, Smile reflects our Caring to Others, Smiling is Funny, Smiling is out of the Ordinary, Smiling is Welcoming."

Smiling is the most beautiful and expressive thing done by humans. Smiling makes us feel good about others and ourselves. Each time you smile, you feel a sense of pleasure, enjoyment and happiness. A friend recently had Botox from an incompetent doctor who injected her in a place that froze her smile. She said, "Even though I look just awful, the worst thing about it, is that I am unable to smile. I miss it so much." Luckily it did disappear after four terrible months.

So be happy and smile!

What is better than having a great belly laugh? When I do have one, I thank the person who brought it on because it feels oh so good. Do you notice how kids or teenagers laugh at everything? They think the smallest thing is funny, giggling all the way. There was a time that I would get the giggles in the most inappropriate places, such as a holy place or other quiet settings, finding it impossible to stop giggling. A person can be crying with tears and heartache and nothing can stop them from grieving more than a good laugh.

As we live life, less will strike us funny. When we find a person or a movie that makes us laugh, it is a wonderful treat. I am fortunate to have a girlfriend with a wonderful sense of humor. We talk several times a week on the phone and invariably she gives me a good laugh. Find people who make you laugh, smile and giggle, they are not that easy to come by.

Senses of humor greatly differ. I love seeing a couple who can sit and smile and laugh together; I consider that to be a terrific relationship. Women love men who are fun and funny. It is not easy to find a person who we can bounce off of using each others sense of humor. It is hard to turn down a friend who brings smiling and laughter into our lives. It is a lot more difficult to date a person from a foreign country who does not speak English as their sense of humor usually differs from ours even if we are trying to speak each others languages. What I think is funny or will set me off laughing may be serious to you. We never know where or when we are about to laugh at and why they say, "It might strike you funny."

On the same token in the movie theaters watching a serious film, I find it offensive when those around me are laughing.

I dislike canned laughter; I immediately shut off a show where the laughter is canned never understanding how the masses accept it. It is planned, not spontaneous and false. Laughter has to be spontaneous, not told by the producer who holds up flags at a canned television show of when to laugh and applaud.

What is sweeter than a baby smiling and laughing at you? We want to keep doing what we are doing to make the baby smile and laugh more. What is sadder than a child who does not smile or laugh?

A false laugh infuriates me. Those who laugh at everything you say by thinking they are supporting you are easy to catch onto. Knowing someone well and recognizing their false laugh sounds quite phony. My brother flew to an important meeting for a job and when he got off of the plane his suitcase with his perfect interview suit was lost. He was horrified and had to run around a strange city in the early morning to find suitable clothing. It was exhausting and he was panicked to get to the meeting in time. After much stress he made it and was at last called in for the interview. The first words out of his mouth were:

"How do I look?"

It broke the ice, he told his story, they all laughed out loud and yup he got the job!

According to *Paul E. McGhee, Ph. D.,* "Your sense of humor is one of the most powerful tools you have to make certain that your daily mood and emotional state support good health. Surround yourself with people that make you happy. Laughter is strong medicine for mind and body.

SOME RECOMMENDATIONS FOR YOU

- Smile, smile, smile!
- Smiling will change your face and make you look younger. It will make the people around you happy.
- Laugh as long and as often as you can from your heart.
- Choose friends who make you happy and who bring out your smile; nothing does it quite so well as a new love affair.

QUESTIONS FOR PERSONAL REFLECTION

1. Do you hide your laugh in order not to sound loud or screeching?
2. Are you a smiler, giving warmth to the world?
3. When did you have your last belly laugh?
4. What makes you smile? A film, a painting, your family, chocolate? Do more of what makes you smile or laugh. Be with people who make you smile and laugh.

Think positive and enjoy your life with many Ha Ha's!

Notes

Part 3

Sex • Friendship
Money

25

Sex

What's It All About Anyway?

S ex is fun. Your body slips into positions you did not dream possible, you feel alive, connected, happy and afterwards hopefully peaceful. Some say sex is highly overrated: "If I never had it again it would be fine with me!" Some say it's delicious, the perfect flavor, and some say pass the vibrator; men are off limits for me.

Growing up in the 50's, stroking and kissing was acceptable, but going all the way was reserved for those known as having "a bad reputation." Remaining true to my good girl image I married as a virgin. Learning everything about sex from my husband and considering my sex life to be fun, exciting and fulfilling is not what led us to divorce; other reasons came into play.

Now was my opportunity after our separation to go back in spirit to nineteen years old, my marital age, and relive my teenage years. It was then that the younger man-older woman dynamic became a possibility and gave me even more opportunities in the dating world. Now I could choose a young guy—the same age I would have chosen at nineteen. I lost out on nothing; I could start all over and I did.

Traveling the world, meeting handsome young men, not considering a trip complete without a love affair was the way to go. Making up for my teenage years by having sexual experiences that I considered love, brought out emotions in me that I did not know existed. Finding out that single women can flirt, love, be aggressive, have a younger partner, have sex and be as wild as we want to be was totally exciting. Love affairs on the road were the way to go; no commitment, great travel stories and for the most part, over at the end of the trip. With those who I did see after a trip, it simply was not the same.

At the age of sixty-nine, I reached the height of my sexual freedom. What brought me to this peak? Perhaps it was my partner allowing me to be all I could be or perhaps I had arrived at a place within my own self, where I could leave my inhibitions behind and be sexually free.

"You are such a slut," he said, one passionate evening, which I considered the highest compliment a nice Jewish girl could receive!

He had a way of making me feel uninhibited. For instance, I would dance for him while he sat in a chair with his legs crossed, focused on my every move. There was no judgement, no matter what silliness I dreamed up for us. He was able to show that he loved and enjoyed being with me, enhancing my sexual responses to him.

Most women have had to deal with a man who couldn't get or keep an erection. I have been with men during my journey with whom I had to struggle to give an erection which was neither fun or sexy; just thoroughly exhausting; it was also emotional trying not to hurt the poor guy's ego. Then there was the passionless man, going through the act, hardly knowing you were there which was even more painful if there was once passion. The hurt of your lover suddenly turning off and lying next to you limp were nights I wanted to forget. One guy nearly fell asleep on my thighs, another rolled over and slept on the floor. One was completely bored trying to stimulate me, looking the other way at the wall, rather than at me, as his hand tried to help him out. At the end of that love affair, I left him with the bitter words, "You were the worst lover I have ever had."

Viagra has come around just in time to save the older generation and while men might have difficulty with an erection most can now be assured that they will be able to perform to some satisfaction. However, plenty of older gentlemen function just fine.

I once asked a 74-year-old male friend, "Do you want to keep on having sex or do you think you had enough?" He looked at me as if to say, am I going to eat tomorrow? "Of course I want to keep having sex," he said. "Sex is good, it is important, it clears the brain."

Love after fifty can be more passionate and more fun than young love. For one thing, experience has taught us the tricks and a woman can be brought to physical heights she never knew existed. One man friend told me he brought a woman to tears; another to her knees begging for more. (I guess I will have to try him out.) The women he described were all well into their sixties. Many women have lived suppressed lives, possibly sharing their life with a selfish man, and are shocked to find out how their bodies can feel and perform with a new and expert lover. Nothing can beat the excitement and passion two people can bring to one another at any age.

Your age or past marital status doesn't have to affect your sex life negatively. Dr. Phil recently had on a divorced woman of about sixty who had found a cool boyfriend; they were living in a tent happy as could be. Her three daughters loved their mom, but were worried that she was not acting appropriately. They wanted her to live in a proper house and to be given the finer things in life. In my opinion, their mom was more enlightened than her kids or Dr. Phil, because she was being fulfilled in ways her daughters or Dr. Phil could never imagine. Doing something untraditional was the icing on the cake of her life. The lesson being, make sure you're living your life for you. And that means sex as well.

I have always held the man responsible for how a woman reacts to him as it is the man who makes the woman come alive. When women complain they do not have orgasms or report that they recite a song or such during love making, or pray for it to be over, it is usually because of the man. He may be inexperienced, overconfident or simply selfish. Some women married their first lover and do not know any better. If they never divorce or are widowed they may never know any better.

WHAT TO DO:

- Women who have not experienced a climax need to tell and teach their partners. Women have to take control and tell the truth to their partners. Some women might be afraid to insult the man they are with and would rather fake an orgasm or not have one. This is ultimately unhealthy for everyone involved.
- Married women can rekindle their sex lives with their mates by learning new ways to rejuvenate themselves. Changing how you look and dress is a big step. Candlelight dinners and music to set the mood always works. Try the motel in the next town or go to a sex therapist if help is needed. Want to turn him on? Call him out of the blue

at work and tell him something naughty and hang up quickly. Keep interrupting his day with sexual remarks and ideas teasing and having fun. "I am already dressed in a short little robe and all bare underneath. I have been vibrating this afternoon but need you to help bring me the height like you always do, you devil." You can certainly be much more wildly creative. Email is great as well but make sure you typed in his address correctly so that it goes only to him.

- There are plenty of ways to spice up a dull sex life and see your partner in a new way. Sex toys are great and sex stores are filled with every gadget imaginable. Now you can even order items online with no embarrassment. Go shopping with your partner; show him what is available; he may learn a thing or two. Watch out! You can get as attached to a vibrator as you can to a man. Teach your partner how to work it or better still, let him watch you as you work it. Some men take offense, "I am here; put that thing away, you don't need it, you got me." Some men are still in the dark about the power of the not knowing that a woman reaches her highest and best climax through her clitoris. Show him how it works! Other men do like toys; one guy left it for me on my pillow before he left in the morning which I thought was extremely cool.

- Couples can become lazy. "I'm not in the mood, not tonight dear." It is understandable that after many years of lovemaking with the same partner it could become boring and tiresome; many married men and women resort to having affairs or not having sex and living as companions; many marriages end up this way. Perhaps at this point an open marriage or love affair might be considered, though it is not my recommendation.

I thought the following article was well defined, noting the difference between clitoral and vaginal orgasm. *Originally Published: December 23, 1994- Last Updated/Reviewed On: July 20 '12 Ask Alice.*

There are many factors that contribute to how an orgasm feels. One variable is the type of physical stimulation, and to what body parts. A "vaginal orgasm" is the notion that women can have an orgasm through stimulation during intercourse or other vaginal penetration, entirely without clitoral stimulation. However, the vagina has few nerve endings, and therefore cannot create an orgasm on its own. Instead of thinking of the vagina and clitoris as separate entities, try thinking about them as a network of nerves and muscles.

In reality, total separation between the vagina and clitoris mostly artificial, and often based on a misunderstanding of what, where, and how big the clitoris really is. The clitoral organ system actually surrounds the vagina, urethra and anus. Rather than thinking of an orgasm as "vaginal" or "clitoral", it makes more sense to think of orgasm in terms of the feelings that came along with it. In the end, an orgasm is an orgasm is an orgasm!

Stimulating the clitoris and (for some women) pressure in or around the vagina can cause pelvic fullness and body tension to build up to a peak. During sexual excitement, the clitoris swells and changes position. The blood vessels through the whole pelvic area also swell, causing engorgement and a feeling of fullness and sexual sensitivity. The inner vaginal lips swell and change shape, and the vagina balloons upward, causing the uterus to shift position. Orgasm is the point at which all the tension is suddenly released in a series of involuntary and pleasurable muscular contractions in the vagina, uterus, and/or rectum.

You or a partner can stimulate your clitoris in a number of different ways — by rubbing, sucking, body pressure, or using a vibrator. Although some women touch the glans of the clitoris to become aroused, for others it can be so sensitive that direct touching hurts, even with lubrication. Also, focusing directly on the clitoris for a long time may cause the pleasurable sensations to disappear.

Your clitoris can also be stimulated during sexual intercourse, most often with the woman on top — this happens when the clitoris is rubbed against the man's pubic bone. It can also be achieved when the man is on top if the man positions himself high enough so that his pubic bone presses against his partner's clitoral area. You or your partner can also stimulate your clitoris with fingers during intercourse to help bring you to orgasm.

Aside from clitoral stimulation, it is important to remember another major organ involved with orgasm — the brain! Emotions, perceptions, memories, and senses determine how we experience sex, rather than past experiences or physical appearance alone. Mental (cortical) stimulation, where the imagination stimulates the brain, can actually help set off an orgasm. Relaxing and concentrating on sensations (rather than worrying about how you're doing) can help your brain process your pleasure.

Overall, orgasms are a very individualistic thing — there is no one correct pattern of sexual response. Whatever works, feels good, and makes you feel more alive and connected with your body (and partner if you have one) are what count!"

- It has been said that every woman has the love life she wants to have. Every woman who truly wants a man can have one. Men are waiting for us at any age and, quite frankly, the most unappealing of women and men have admirers. For the most part, if a woman keeps herself in good shape, good health, and keeps her mind occupied, there is no cap on age to having love affairs or enjoying your spouse. Men don't look at women like we women look at women. Men simply do not care if you change your hair style, put on a few pounds or have wrinkles. I once went away with a man and went into the bathroom with my own hair but came out wearing a long wig. This quite attentive man never even noticed. Another man who likes to take women on cruises told me that he always takes an inside room. I asked him why. "Some ladies," as he called us women, "who are not in the best of shape would rather have darkness day and night; that way there are no limitations on our love life." Love can be practical and sexy at the same time. If you have never been in an inside room on a ship, they are pitch black.

- Men are there for us to love and to love us. There is truly someone for everyone. There are even men out there who are waiting for the suppressed, needful woman. This breed of man has no age or beauty restrictions; they simply love women and consider it to be their role in life, no matter their own age, to be that of a lover. This breed of lover is usually uncommitted. They have studied women as one studies other subjects, knowing a woman's needs and wants. These men might not stick around for a long time but each woman will have gained from knowing him. If he comes your way, grab him to be sexually happy, have fun and companionship. For his own personal reasons of fear and abandonment, he keeps things loose. He might be of a certain age where commitment is all too much for him but more than that this type of man does not want the responsibility of taking care of a woman in any other way than to satisfy her sexually. He is a man who wants to have a good time and he has chose you to have a good time with, so enjoy. Be sexy, be fun, be frivolous, be smart by giving him space and time away. If you want something more from him it probably will not work. However, If he is of an older age (70 plus) he might want to settle down, although a leopard does not change his spots and it will be only a matter of time until he will be adding on someone new or leaving you behind or at the very least carry on with flirtations. His way of life is in his blood but I have learned to enjoy such a man as a treat, an interlude in my life.

Then there is the torture of forbidden love that fills your mind body, and soul, the one where one would give up everything they have for the other person, even family, the need for the other person so overwhelming.

FOR THOSE WHO HAVE GIVEN UP:

Many women, both married and single resort to making their lives happy in other ways by filling their time with activities, girlfriends, their children and grandchildren. A friend divorced in her sixties. She was through; she closed up shop, leaving sex out of her new single life. "I am not interested in a man; no men for me." Perhaps her feelings were caused by a bad marriage, a selfish mate or her own attitude towards sex. She may not feel sexually appealing or does not want to compete with other women. She has found other ways to live a good life in a different way than being with a man. Perhaps she is more of a serious nature, not looking for a quick interlude. This particular woman has a full life unto her self; never home, loves cards, vacations and has an abundance of girlfriends with whom she shares her life, along with her wonderful family. One beautiful woman married three times prefers to knit and watch television and have people visit, another visits friends, travels and still works; all void of sex.

WE CAN HAVE IT ALL:

It only takes one to get you started. When was the last time that your heart fluttered at the sight of your man? Have you ever seen a stranger across the room and felt so drawn to him or her that it has paralysed you; or not being able to get the word hello out of your mouth? Has your heart ever beaten so fast and hard that you thought it would burst? Has your heart ever beaten so fast because of a disappointment in love that you thought it would burst? Passion does wild things to us and we must never give up the thought that it can happen to us for as long as we live. There is no such thing as too old, unappealing. In my singing class yesterday, a woman well into her eighties sang out with unbelievable gust and passion, "I still love you so," making me gasp. My sister tells a story of meeting a woman in San Miguel, Mexico, who after years of acting as a doting grandma, took off for one year to discover herself. She met men, went to their famous library, corresponded with her grandchildren and family but welcomed sex as well. So let's go out and meet these potential falling to our knees men.

We no longer have to wait to be introduced by a friend or wait for one of our friend's husbands to die; men are all over and they are looking for you.

ONLINE DATING IS TERRIFIC! Why not try it if you have not already? It is simple and easy. Before you know it, you will have many proposals for a date; You will be getting dressed up in a different manner than going out with the girls and rushing to buy new makeup. You will be excited to meet him with the hope of engaging in a good conversation. It does not have to work out especially if you are a woman who has been married with children. Grant you, some women need to be taken care of for financial reasons. "When I put up my photo and write something clever and tell my real age I get many responses. I might do that for a month at a time, stopping, and later picking it up again, depending on the responses I get. I have met some great guys on free sites like "Craigslist." I have found that there is no real difference in who you meet if you pay money to meet someone or if you sign up for free. You will still have to weed out the undesirables. In fact, quality men often test out a free site before committing to an agreement or serious dating. I also like the site "Senior People Meet."

MY ADVICE FOR POSTING A DATING PROFILE OR PERSONALS AD:
- It is important to set your goals for both yourself and who you might attract. Are you looking for a rich man? Handsome and charming? Professional? A traveler or simply a good companion?

- If you are seeking marriage, say so! If you are seeking sex, say so.
- State the ages of the men you desire and state your age as well. This is important rather than having to admit something you lied about later on.
- Keep your options open by dating outside your race, perhaps, or someone from another country.
- When you find someone you like, meet up right away. Some men put off a meeting, not wanting to take a chance on buying a woman a drink that might turn out to be a disaster. If he prefers not to take the chance and likes schmoozing on the phone better, I move on or invite him. Life's too short.
- If I have enjoyed the company of a man who has not called me again, I call him. Nobody likes waiting by the phone, and some men prefer to be chased. One man I know writes something lovely to me after we see each other, but he does not call again. I have learned to call him. This is just how he operates. It does not bother me in the least because when I call he is receptive and we go out and have a good time. However, if you do make the call, be prepared, he truly might not have been interested in you.

HERE ARE SOME OTHER TIPS

- Miscommunication is always a hazard in dating. One friend would have missed out on marriage if she had not followed up with a man she liked. Her motto became, "Call, call, call." We women have to remember how fragile men's egos are and while it is wonderful to be perused, if there is a guy that you like why not do a little work yourself?
- Ask a man for his card right up front so you have his information in case anything happens and you say goodbye without exchanging numbers. Opportunities do pass and there were times that I returned to the same spot hoping I might run into that certain someone again and invariably never finding him.

- Some men shower you with attention, call at any given hour wanting long conversations, others give a hard time, disappear, keep you guessing; if you can, go with the flow. If you have had a good time together, he will be back, almost certainly.

- A first date should be upbeat leaving out troubles or illness or rambling on about the wonderful things you did or didn't do in your life. Please don't discuss exes in any size shape or manner. Stating you were once married is all you need to say. Later in life dating carries baggage and nobody wants to hear sad stories either. Be interested in him as most men need attention and usually love the focus to be on him. Be caring and genuinely interested in the person. Be sexual by being flirtatious if he is of interest to you. There are many more men than women so even if you are a femme fatale you might still be in for some surprises. Most of all be yourself. Every relationship is different. Each person brings out different parts of us to explore and there is no end to the intimacy that can be shared between two people. Identifying your goals will help you decide how to approach love and sex. I consider myself independent; therefore, my main goal at this time of my life is to have a good time. Nothing pleases me more than laughing and having fun during sex. A smart man knows that women like to have fun, like to feel flattered and made to feel like a Princess or perhaps at this stage of life a Queen by being complimented, treated with respect and we women should settle for nothing less. As stated before, my attractive friend in great shape with stage talent is seventy years old and has never married until now proving it is never too late. When my grandmother married at eighty-two for the third time; her husband was seventy-nine, we kids asked, "Do you think they are going to have sex?" We will never know the answer but if I follow in her footsteps you can be sure that this grandmother will and hopefully so will you.

Look how free our society is becoming: men can marry men, women can marry women. Black and white couples are becoming common. When I crossed the racial barrier for the first time, seven years ago I told him "You are the first black man I have ever been interested in." I am sure that handsome charming man heard that story before. Recently I drove through the southern part of South Carolina on an early Sunday morning and stopped in to a Church Service. There I saw two interracial couples and I thought, wow, South Carolina, you have come a long way. Yet we still have a long way to go. Same-sex couples, as well as couples with large age differences, face discrimination today.

NOW YOU HAVE INVITED HIM IN:

Some men believe that coming on strong is the way to go. I have found that when the man's lips and his manhood are ready and waiting so when I lean over or fall into his arms, passion will be at its best. When a man allows a woman to come to him, he will have the best sex; it is always the woman's choice. In the beginning a man should wait for the woman to be ready; once that happens and you enjoy each other, then we love a take-charge man.

What about after sex? I prefer a man who goes home after our evening together. There was a time that I might have been insulted: love me and then leave me? Now that I have been single for almost half of my life, I enjoy sleeping alone. One man said, to me after a wonderful evening together, "I hope you don't mind, but I am going to get up and go home." I am sure he thought I was going to be upset. Instead I said, "That is fine with me," thinking to myself, "what a blessing." It is all about what we get used to and later on that particular man and I travelled together so there was no going home and that was great too.

Go out and find that person who will stimulate you, who you will want to spend time with and maybe even fall in love; take a chance.

The bottom line is that there is plenty of time in life for card games, grandchildren and a new date. Try one out, just once.

SOME RECOMMENDATIONS FOR YOU

- Try going from grandma to hot lover in one night. If the younger people in the audience has questioned if older people have sex, the answer is, "We Do!"
- Live single, live married. Many women have three or four marriages, each spouse bringing a whole new experience and lifestyle. If you want a new man go get him. Make it your goal. With the Internet at your fingertips there's an endless supply of men to meet.
- Your sexual parts, barring illness, should work well into old age and you are entitled to the joy of sex. There are no excuses for not at least thinking about passion and bringing it into or back into your life.
- Some women complain about dryness and the loss their libido as they pass menopause. Dryness can be cured by lubricating creams; there are many books about enjoying sex through out your life. Read as many self-help books about this. As for the libido, all it takes is that one man to bring us women back to life again.
- Become assertive if shyness has held you back. The simple magic word to meeting someone is, "Hello."
- Remember that everyone has different needs and tastes.
- There is someone for everyone, especially you.
- Flirtation is rewarding in itself. With some women it might be all she needs.

QUESTIONS FOR PERSONAL REFLECTION

1. Have you closed up shop, thinking sex is something in your past?
2. Are you fiery and ready to go but think you will never meet anyone?
3. Do you feel that you are no longer attractive to a man? Why? If you think it is true, will you try to change your image?
4. Are you eager to meet someone but don't know how to go about it?
5. Are you waiting for someone to knock on your door and if he does, fine, and if he does not that is fine too? Why not be more assertive if the latter is the case?
6. Have you tried online dating? If not will you try for the heck of it? A great relationship can happen at any age. For me I can honestly say that fifty was fabulous, sixty was sensational and seventy sizzles!
7. Have you tried it but feel unsuccessful? Can you change your requirements realizing there are different needs at different times?

Let us hope that we all have the opportunity to have our hearts broken. Love makes us feel alive, over the top with meaning.

Notes

26

When Sex It Is Not Wanted

Ouch!

Persistent genital arousal disorder; my personal story:
After menopause a very strange thing happened to me. My libido sped up to the point of driving me out of my mind. This excruciating feeling, a hardening of the clitoris that had to be released, caused severe pain, anxiety, frustration and horror and would not leave me until I relieved myself. This feeling would attack me at the most unusual of places: a bus, a family outing, a walk, and I would never know when it would hit. I could be fine one minute and the next minute for absolutely no reason, my own body would go out of control. There were times I would compare myself with a mad dog in heat. There was no calming it down. The only relief I could get was through masturbation and I could never do it enough. I developed a pattern of this feeling hitting me every third day and would plan my day ahead so I could be somewhere private. I visited doctors, several OB-GYN and not one had a clue how to help me. I wrote to sex therapists and they had no clue either. I was in this alone, helpless, not daring to mention it to anyone as it was far too

humiliating. When I tried telling a friend or two they thought I was oversexed, a nymphomaniac and thought it would be great if it happened to them. Doctors were embarrassed when I described my condition even though when they examined me they could see a swelling in my clitoris, almost to be compared with a man's erection. It was impossible to get through to anyone. It had nothing to do with a man or for him being the answer to my satisfaction. The last thing I wanted was a man, my desire was insatiable. I used a vibrator and went through boxes and boxes of batteries. I would run to sex stores to find the right toy for me and when they were out of stock on the one that satisfied me, I would become insane. I knew every sex store in a forty-mile radius. One climax was never enough, I would have to have at least twelve to twenty-four leaving me utterly exhausted and relieved for three days. There was no help out there. I took baths, I meditated, I tried anything and everything to calm me down but nothing would stop the attacks. My condition went on for years and years; it was so horrific that I began to think I could not go on living this way. It was a feeling of being frustrated sexually all the time, much like when you are stimulated and are unable to climax. The pain and sensitivity was excruciating.

After suffering for years I read an article that anti depressants cause men to lose their sexual urge and erection. I thought maybe that could work for me. I made an appointment with a therapist and told her my story. She prescribed Paxil and after taking it for about a month it kicked in. I could not believe that it was working. I was normal; the relief was incredible. I have tested myself without Paxil and even after so many years, my body begins to get that insane feeling.

Many years later, I mentioned my condition to another friend and she described the same symptoms. She would have to pull to the side of the road and relieve herself; it would hit her just as it did me. Paxil brought her great relief too.

While some of my readers might think this is an exciting thing to happen, it was far from sexual; it was painful, humiliating and had nothing whatsoever to do with passion or sex.

In the years that followed a few articles began to appear and the condition was named. It is called PGAD, Persistent Genital Arousal Disorder.

I added this to my book for the main reason that if you are suffering as I did, you now have support. Please read below:

Persistent Genital Arousal Disorder (PGAD), originally called Persistent Sexual Arousal Syndrome (PSAS) also known as Restless Genital Syndrome (ReGS or RGS) In addition to being very rare, the condition is also frequently unreported by sufferers who may consider it shameful or embarrassing. It results in a spontaneous, persistent, and uncontrollable genital arousal in women, with or without orgasm. Physical arousal caused by this syndrome can be very intense and persist for extended periods, days or weeks at a time. Orgasm can sometimes provide temporary relief, but within hours the symptoms return. The return of symptoms, is sudden and unpredictable. Failure or refusal to relieve the symptoms can be debilitating, preventing concentration on mundane tasks. Some situations, such as riding in an automobile or train vibrations from mobile phones, and even going to the toilet can aggravate the syndrome unbearably causing the discomfort to verge on pain. Antidepressants, antiandrogenic agents, and anesthetizing gels offer relief and in my case cure. Psychotherapy with cognitive reframing of the arousal as a healthy response may also be used.

SOME RECOMMENDATIONS FOR YOU.

- If you have experienced this, visit a psychiatrist and talk to them about this. Bring in articles from the internet supporting what you are saying. When it happened to me there was no such thing.

QUESTIONS FOR PERSONAL REFLECTION

1. Have you had this experience?
2. Have you ever heard of it?
3. Are you suffering in the dark with nowhere to turn?

There is help out there for you who suffer.

Notes

27

Friends

Too Many? Not Any?

"My friend, my confidant, always there like magic, to remind me, how lucky I am, to have such a good friend, someone who believes in me, even when I don't, words to encourage, give me hope, and then there was the laughter we shared," written to me by my friend Clara.

Are you a social butterfly with many friends, or are you a person who cherishes one or two close pals? Friendship is wonderful, though, like love, it is not always easy. Friendships demand time and effort, requiring us to put our needs aside to support another person. A 2006 study found that people living in the United States had fewer friends than ever, with one in four Americans claiming they had no one to confide in. According to Kornblum, "It can be hard to meet the people who would make the perfect friend. Human beings can clash very easily, which is why it's hard for some people to maintain friendships. Friendship is based on need. Some simply need more friends to function, while others enjoy their alone time almost as much—or more than—they like the company of others. However, we all need at least some sort of friendship in our lives."

Enjoying your own company is a gift to yourself that not all possess. Some people simply cannot be alone; resorting to the sound of TV or other background noise. Silence is their biggest fear.

FRIENDSHIP NEEDS

Friends are blessed people and friendship is a vital component of our lives. When you have been down in the dumps or are unsure of how to handle a situation, isn't it a true blessing to call a friend and get their support and sound advice without judgment? Friends listen to our stories, our good news and bad; they act as our therapists, listening to our same stuff endlessly. We learn through the years that we are not as unique as we think we are. Our joys and sorrows are much the same. Most importantly, in the end we learn that our answers truly lie within. We don't need many friends; three are great but one good one will suffice. For me, my need has been to have fewer friends in my single life. I've enjoyed the exploration of myself after marriage, by traveling, dating and being independent. A lady who lunches has never been my style, nor am I a woman who enjoys shopping or going out on errands with a girlfriend.

On the flip side, there have been times that I needed a friend and no one was around. I visited my therapist as it was troubling to me. "This has been your choice," he said. "You live your life by filling it with activities that do not involve other people, preferring to do them alone, being alone. Therefore, if you suddenly want company it might not happen." He went on to say, "This has been your path and it's needless to feel sad about it"

After realizing how right he was, I have learned to appreciate being with friends and my alone time without reservation.

NO FRIENDS RIGHT NOW?

Spending endless time alone is usually not a good thing, even if you prefer to be alone. It can isolate far too much, as it is a human need to be loved and feel loved. It may be time to reach out to a new friend who might also be a young child to mentor, doing charity work, joining an organization, or learning something new in a class. It is comforting bouncing ideas or thoughts off another person, as it makes some of life's decisions with all the twists and turns easier.

We begin by cooing at each other in our mothers' carriages, stroking one another as we play, fascinated by each other's faces. Then it becomes "Mine, mine," stating our power and control over the world, bringing our little playmates to tears. Even as we hurt the feelings of others and vice versa, we still need one another. Just as we learn as infants to share, it is essential that we continue to share throughout our lives with family and friends. Friends introduce us to other friends and we connect our friends to their friends and the circle grows. Some introduce business partners or mates, and some are matchmakers. Have you ever introduced two friends to each other only to forget when the two of them bonded? "Mine, mine," comes back into play, selfishly leaving the other person out.

Friends come to us differently through the different stages of our lives. There were our wonderful school friends who we can now find on Facebook, reuniting with some. There are websites set up in most cities to find friends you might have lost. Then came the incredible bonding that came with raising our children friends, the friends who heard your babies cry and play and who might be doing the same with you now if you are first experiencing a new child. There were our newlywed friends as we entered into marriage. But most important there were the friends we had fun with, the ones who heard our arguments, who shared our joys and sorrow. Then if we were married with children and divorced or widowed, we made new single friends replacing our mates to share our new dates, jobs, Mah Jongg, cards, temple, church, an activity, a class, a sport, a game, role model friends opening our minds to participate in the arts, and those showing us how to spiritually grow.

Single people need friends to keep them going and just as importantly, so do married people to keep them going. My ex-husband did not like to be involved with any friends; he wanted me all to himself and discouraged friendships, causing me to feel lonely. I marveled at the couples who seemingly were having a good time vacationing together, going to restaurants and having fun, watching my neighbor's active house of friends coming and going. I often thought that maybe our marriage would have been more fulfilling had our social life been better. Interestingly enough, after divorce he became a social butterfly and I went from social butterfly to being more of a loner. Perhaps he did not like my choice of friends. In suburban life the woman usually plans the dates or maybe it had to be his idea with his choice of people.

LEARNING TO BE A GOOD FRIEND

Yes, friends are wonderful but they just don't fall into our laps and stay. Like anything else in life we have to learn and practice to be a good friend and sometimes it takes a great deal of patience. We choose our friends, not our family, and sometimes our choices may not work out. To keep a friend we must be sympathetic to their needs as well as our own.

Think about what you want out of a friendship. Friends come in many sizes, shapes and characters and these sizes shapes and characters bring out our characters. A genuine person who tells the truth is high on my list, as well as one who is kind, sincere, trustworthy, thoughtful, vibrant, smiles often, and is real. Honesty is extremely important when asked even if it means hearing something I don't want to know. How else can one grow? But then again, how much honesty and openness do you want in a friendship? Still, the friends I enjoy the most are my confidants with whom I share honesty and openness.

Hearing great news from my friends makes me happy and bad news needs my tender loving care. I love giving advice. Just ask my kids! When I disclose myself it is a great feeling to hear my friend open up about him/herself. I opened up to a friend about a family matter never thinking she was in the same boat as she seemed on such good terms with her family. What I thought about her life was not true and we entered a soulful conversation, supporting one other.

It is true that some people are not good for us. It is also true that we sometimes need to learn lessons from that person, while considering the opportunity to learn more about ourselves, even when the news might not be positive. Then it is time to examine ourselves to see if we might have been the cause. When we are hurt by a friend repeatedly it is time to move on. I am thankful for the difficult people who have challenged me and taught me how to handle new or strange situations. They brought out that new growth in me.

Parents can often choose good friends for their children. It's the best way for the continuation of friendship; I know this to be true as I chose two friends for my kids that have remained always in their lives. Some friends remain in our lives for all of our lives even though that is not particularly the norm. In my case my childhood friends and the friends that I had bringing up children are my true lasting friends. I am fortunate to have two childhood friends who leave little room for any secrets or lies. They are my unconditional friends, friends I can call on any hour of the day. While most women consider their mates their best friends, nothing can ever beat us girlfriends. I often say, to keep our friendships, 'We simply have to put up with each others' neuroses!"

Friendship must be learned like anything else and sometimes we have to repeat the same lessons until we learn how to become a better friend. How do we do it? By listening more, calling more, inviting more, rather than waiting for the other person to contact you. Some of us stand on ceremony, waiting for the other person to make a move. "It was their turn," or having feelings of insecurity that the other person is not fond of you. Never assume what another person is feeling or thinking because most times we are wrong or simply do not know. Try to take the initiative even if it does not work out. Waiting for one of my kids to call has built up much steam in me. "Call your mother" doesn't always work. I find it might be me who needs to do the calling. Holding grievances and losing a friend because of some inner conflict that belongs only to you needs to be addressed. To be a good friend, kindness and caring is essential.

Then there are friendships that can be draining and sometimes we have to set boundaries and tell friends that we can no longer listen to them endlessly or have them knock on our door at any given time.

Do you think a friend should tell you if they see your spouse out with another woman? It's a tricky question. Personally I do not, as chances are the couple will rebound; it also gives the friend who tells you about yourself power, as she now has you at her mercy. She now is part of your pain. I am suggesting that you mind your own business. I was devastated when my best friend told me about another woman she had seen with my guy. Not only did she tell me, she described them holding hands, her hands slipped into his back pocket. Ouch, ouch. Our friendship dissolved based on other reasons as well.

Friends are to be cherished but they need to cherish us too. They can hurt us deeply and disappoint. At age fourteen, I was dumped by a friend. One of my three best friends borrowed my suitcase and when she did not return it for a long while, words started to fly between us and we stopped talking to each other. My other two friends took her side and all three snubbed me. I was heartbroken, watching them pass my house on the way to our usual Saturday afternoon movie and outing. It was my first taste of terrible loneliness and rejection until we finally made up. I still question to this day if I was the one at fault.

I once asked a friend to give me a ride home. She told me, "Just take my car, I don't have time to drive you." I had no way to return her car and would have been in the same situation.

Recently I was in Florida, where I had lived for many years. I had nowhere to sleep for a couple of nights as the hotel I was in was full. I mentioned this to my friends. Not one invited me to stay even though their apartments were expansive and I had entertained them lavishly in my home for weekends at a time. I moved into an unfurnished apartment for three nights and asked to borrow a sheet and pillow. One kind friend brought it to me; the rest said without any remorse, "Kmart sells inexpensive things." I don't think any of them realized how terrible they made me feel. Another friend said, "You should not have asked and set yourself up for disappointment." Certainly another way to look at it. Each of us has tremendous power to hurt others.

In my younger years, I made a tennis date with a girlfriend. I rushed from my home to meet her, after working hard to get a babysitter. There she was, playing with three other women, completely leaving me out of the game. I was devastated by her behavior at the time and it ended our friendship; she felt no remorse. We don't realize how much pain we can bring to another person with a simple word or act. When one lacks self-esteem, self-growth, or insecurity, and a friend is contrary or preying on weaknesses or vulnerability, we can lose out on beautiful thoughts and ideas by not having the right support and sometimes the push we need for greater things.

Sadly, as life barrels down the highway, we leave friends behind. It is heartbreaking to part with a friend we love. I remember sharing my life as a new wife and mother with my dear friend. Then her husband changed locations and moved his family to another state. I have a vivid memory to this day, more than fifty years ago, of watching their car drive away. How could I go on? Life was no longer fun; I cried into my husband's arms.

At one time I had four best girl friends. It has been said that relationships are not meant to last and that might be true. Friendship is based on need and sometimes we tend to move on when conversations slow down or good times seem nonexistent. The important thing is to know we had a good friend that we loved and cherished and not to part as enemies when the relationship has ended. Always keep the door open, as life takes us in many directions. While you might need to part from a friend, for months or even for years, there may be a time that the friendship can be renewed in a different way. Why did these friendships end, I might be asked? So many variable reasons that equalled selfishness, disappointment, moving away, or outgrowing a person from both sides. It is best to put our past relationships in a different place in our hearts and to stay in touch now and then. However, there are the friends with whom we must make a complete break or they must make a complete break with us.

Throughout life, most of us make friends, keep, or let go of friends, and move on to make other friends. There have been times that I wish I could have an old friend back who I had misunderstood, but that does not easily happen. Either the other person no longer cares or does not believe in forgiveness or has gone in a different direction, making it difficult to go backwards. Should friends come back to us, it is important to start fresh. Do not go over past pains; it will only postpone the joy you can begin to have again with one another.

I recently reunited with a group of friends from the bringing up children era and we had a marvelous lunch together reminiscing. After that day, I reached out but there has been no follow up. The past usually has nothing to do with how we are living our life now, and while it is always wonderful to hear about such a person or to see them again, it usually remains our past. This is not a bad thing as it shows growth into other dimensions of our lives. They say we do not lose friends; we just learn who the real ones are.

Having a friend who is more learned than yourself is a gift. I prefer a person who has unique thoughts, not necessarily book learned, street smart. My mom wanted me to be friends with the smartest girl in our class; I do remember her teaching me the Ouija board, convincing me it was all true. When we meet someone who has our similar ideas or tastes, we bond.

When you are young at heart, your friendships can extend to many ages. Younger friends can gain knowledge from those who are older if they are open minded about age. While we mostly feel comfortable with people our own age as we have gone through the music, the trends, same age children, etc., it is nice to expand to other generations. It is surprising to me how we influence other people, especially when it comes to a young child. A young nephew of mine surprised me when he became an adult telling me he liked listening to my stories at the dinner table when he was a little boy and always looked forward to me coming to the house. I had no idea, not realizing how we influence others.

Can one friend be everything to you or can you be everything to them? It's not possible for any one person to fill all of our needs or for us to fulfill theirs. As said earlier, we also must know who to tell what to, as your heart and soul given to a friend who lacks intimacy and who would prefer to gossip can backfire. We can say one thing to one friend that we dare not say to another. We usually know who will take offense based on their value system and sense of humor.

There is nothing like having a friend who gets it! There are some people who are hard to convince of what we are saying, having to explain what we mean. A sharp friend who can pick things up and be on the same wavelength as you is a treasure. There are couples who say one thing and their partner can finish the sentence. This is what I mean by getting it.

Remember to keep true friends around and let go of false ones or the ones who bring negative energy into your life. Sometimes we have so much love for a friend that it is hard to think they may not be treating us right. We might put up with their nonsense causing us pain because we don't want to let them go! It all comes down to our own self esteem, and at the same time trying to analyze the part we played in the friendship and how we might be at fault. A real friend will not desert you when you are down, and will not become jealous of your accomplishments.

I asked a friend of mine who has a long list of friends beginning from childhood, "How do you manage to have so many good friends?" Her answer was that she is a good listener. However, knowing her as I do, it is more than that! When I talk to her I know that her responses will not only be intelligent but sincere. She is an honest person who tells the truth without judgment and one who is sincerely interested in other people. She is humble about her own accomplishments, recognizing the other person first, joyful about their achievements, not being able to wait to spread the good news. She has the information stored in her head about the good times we shared, and because our relationship is a long one, she can remember our pain as well.

More than anything, it is important to have fun with friends; they bring us joy, making us laugh and cry, jump up and down and often lay us out. Having fun and good times is important to our lives. It is refreshing when mixed with our everyday, sometimes tedious lives. What we consider fun today might not be the same as what we considered fun years ago. For instance, walking through a park and looking at the nature might be more fun today than going to a party. What about you; how do you spell fun today?

WOMEN FRIENDS CAN BE DIFFICULT BECAUSE WE JUST ARE!

Women are jealous creatures by nature and many women have grown bitter over the years. Some enjoy making nasty remarks and gossiping about other friends. Some friends bring out the goodness in us and there are those who bring out our flaws, helping us to grow. It is important to be a good friend, one who we can trust and who can trust us.

Many women complain that in later years it is harder to make friends; people become set in their ways, have their own circle of friends and simply don't want to be bothered forming new friendships. Therefore singles find themselves alone. Women can be difficult; some like it hot, some like it cold, some don't want to take a taxi, a subway, they keep different hours, eat different foods and have their definite likes and dislikes, making it sometimes difficult to bond. My new motto, like I said: "We just have to put up with each others neuroses."

A daughter, after seeing her moms' friends pass away one by one, asked her, "What are you going to do without your friends?" Her mom, at age ninety-two, replied, "Go out and get new ones."

Do your gifts have to equal your friends gifts monetarily? Perhaps you lavished a friend with an expensive gift and received a less costly gift back from them. It honestly does not matter, so long as you were thought about; that is the ultimate gift.

SOME RECOMMENDATIONS FOR YOU

- I no longer seek my friend's or family's approval on my path to good health and new adventures. Some friends have said to me, Well, Carol Sue you are getting older, you need to prepare, do this or that.... hmmmmm, you are getting older, I am getting more vibrant, nature will tell me when it is time, not you. In all honesty, the opportunities only get wilder and vaster because we have more experience, courage, with more new thoughts and ideas.
- Be your own best friend first. You can't take care of a friend otherwise.
- Be around encouraging people who genuinely like you and make you feel good. You know who they are, because you feel good around them.
- Mix with a person that has more aspiration than you and more, or a different type of, intelligence. This is hard to do, but as said, be your own best friend first.
- Stay away from angry people who create doubt in those around them.
- Watch out for those who are kind to you but hostile to others; in the end they will treat you as one of the same.
- When you ask a friend for advice, know that they are coming from their own fears and often their response is based on what they would do in a given situation, rather than considering you. Listen to their advice and make your own decisions.
- Loyalty, honesty and authenticity are essential ingredients for being a friend and that works both ways.

- If you sincerely care for your friend, you can learn to be a good friend by practicing giving and kindness. A good friend will be truthful and honest and stand by you and this too works both ways.
- Learn to apologize and learn how to forgive (before it is too late in your friendship).
- Groups of friends are more important at certain stages of life than at another; there were times we had a crowd, invited in groups to parties, bar mitzvahs, weddings, pool parties sharing our children's accomplishments.
- We have to decide how much time we can give to a needful friend who takes away from your own time; especially one who feels free to knock on your door at any given time.
- Sometimes giving constructive criticism can make a friend understand what she/he needs to learn to improve the friendship. Some friends will not accept any advice; so carefully choose.
- A true friend will not allow you to be insulted or picked on by another when you are in their company.
- A true friend will build your self-esteem and will not be jealous of your accomplishments, but proud of you.
- It is a terrible thing to exclude a friend when others are invited to a group get together.
- Some say life is not worth living without friends.

QUESTIONS FOR PERSONAL REFLECTION

1. Do you consider yourself to be a good friend? Why do you think that you are?
2. Are you a good listener or do you prefer to do the talking leaving little room for an interrupt?
3. Are you easygoing? Do you agree with most suggestions or does it have to be your idea, your way? Why?
4. Are friends important to you or do you prefer to do most things on your own?
5. Have you lost a friend that you loved? Do you know why that person no longer wanted your company?
6. Are you a leader or do you prefer to follow other peoples' suggestions?
7. Have you let go of friends because you did not know how to apologize or communicate properly?
8. Would you like to call that friend today? Will you?

What would we girls do without our girlfriends?

Notes

28

Money

Love and Pesetas

Ihave included money in this part of my book here along
with sex as to some money can be as sexy as sex. How much
money do you think you need to be happy? Is there a magic
number that pops out of your head and do you really think
that if you achieved that number, you would be happier than
you are now? They say anything over $75,000 a year does not
make you any happier. The idea is poverty is no way to live, but
being really filthy rich won't bring you any more happiness or
contentment.

The worst thing a woman can do to herself after divorce is to be
angry and hateful and tie up her life in courts trying to get even
or seeking revenge. If the settlement is fair and if a woman has
enough money to make her life comfortable, go out and start
living instead of fighting the system. Try a new vocation to keep
you grounded or get a part time job if you need to supplement
your income. Whatever you do don't spend your life miserable
fighting for the sake of money and revenge. Be aware of the

girlfriends who tell you to seek revenge as these well-meaning friends may be coming from their own bad experiences. Courts are not amusing and will take years out of your joyful new life. Avoid attorneys and courts at all costs if it is at all possible.

In my case, I knew what my husband earned and I felt that I got a fair share. I remember asking him, "What can I do to help you get over your anger?" We had enough misery before we divorced, didn't we? A good kind spirit will set you apart from the woman who feels there is nothing more ahead except getting even, revenge, taking him for his worth, and dwelling on her past.

How we think about money is a very personal thing and how we spend our money is equally personal. Each one of us has our own set of values about where and how to spend it. We might look at a person and declare them cheap. However, they might be extravagant in ways that you have not realized or where you look cheap.

For instance, the cheapest person I ever met in my life is a friend who simply does not spend any money. Perhaps she has to fill up her car with gas, but not too often, as she does not go far out of her neighborhood. Obviously she has to eat, but will buy chicken parts that are close to being non-edible or buy produce in dollar stores. To me, she is simply cheating her own body. Her water bottle was filled from a bathroom sink while I bought mine from a vendor. Before my eyes and to much amazement the water turned a darkish color; she still drank it. She does not dare to eat in a restaurant and if she accompanies you, she will order a glass of tap water. Her gifts to people are things she found at a thrift store or garage sale which is a kind thought as long as they are in good condition. Is she poor? How could she be, she saves every penny. Does she have to watch her money? Absolutely not. She has always worked and earned money. She is simply cheap. Yet, she is a person who is generous with her time, she thinks nothing of picking you up and driving you to an appointment. However, **she is in love with the money she has in her bank account.**

My parents taught me well about money, learning from my family how to protect my money. They worked in their dress shop and awarded us kids a good life, none of us ever feeling deprived. Going into real estate and making my own money, did not change my lifestyle. Living below my means rather than above was my way to live and still is. For me being forced to have to go to work or heaven forbid being in debt was not worth the new condo. Therefore, living below my means was never a hardship and rather a pleasure. I could come and go as I wished not having to get up with an alarm clock, truly one of my greatest fears in life. If I had taken a nine to five job with a large company, I probably would have been an extremely wealthy filthy rich woman today. There would have been more discipline and support, but working on my own and being independent was more important to me. **I am in love with protecting my money.**

Loving money too much or wanting it too much can lead to an unhappy life. For instance, you might choose money over love, leaving you emotionally void. Yet as the saying goes, why not marry a rich man rather than a poor one? There are women who would not dare to love a poor man as to these women having money is a lot more sexy. **They are in love in an even different way: with their mate's money.**

Women have babies and they have careers. Often they must choose between the two. I see more nannies walking around New York City wheeling baby carriages than I see moms. Children grow up no matter what and women have the power to choose to be a stay at home mom or bring in the money. It might be said that **these women are in love with bringing**

home money for their own self-worth and for the needs of their family.

How much money do you really think you need to get through the rest of your life is another question? Assuming you live comfortably, do you have enough time left to live to spend all of your money? If you are over sixty, probably not. Some of us want to make sure we leave our children money so hold back on our own selves. They would sooner not touch their principal and live off of their income because **they are in love with leaving an inheritance.**

However you display your love for money and your attitude toward it is fine as long as you are not in debt. Live independently and securely living a lifestyle void of worrying about money by accepting what you have. Do what you love to do and money will come. **Be in love with security.**

That said, if you are in debt, do everything and anything to get out of it and start anew. Debt will rule your life. Here is a story:

Two people that I know are pros on how to get out of debt. They suggest above all, to make a firm commitment to get out of debt. They took a stand on cutting back on expenses and finding creative ways to pay debt sooner. By cutting down on everyday expenses and charges, such as restaurants, vacations, clothes, entertainment, newspapers, cable TV, they were able to take that extra money and make mortgage payments each two weeks instead of once a month. If there was extra money they sent more to the company than what was required. When they owned their own home outright, they were able to make their own choices on insurance that the bank previously required ending up in monthly savings plus no more mortgage payments.

Next came their enormous credit card debt as they lived on seven different cards, which they began to pay off one at a time.

They paid the highest rate card with the smallest balance to get rid of that card debt. They kept the card they had just paid off because now they were now able to get a better rate. They were showing good credit.

Then they took their next highest rate and placed it on the credit card offering them a great rate. They paid that one off and kept it to get a better rate and as again they were building good credit. They kept doing this until they ended up with one or two cards that had debt. Once they were paid off, they were able to get a zero rate credit card which they paid off before the interest rate kicked in. They continued to go from card to card to card bringing their debt to zero until they were able to charge without financing. Within five years they were debt-free. Of course the truth is not to ever go into debt that becomes overwhelming.

Where to keep important papers:

I keep a two-drawer file cabinet with bank statement, property owned, leases copies of credit cards, licenses, etc.

I have a safe deposit box to keep any papers that are important to me such as my will, power of attorney, living will. A safe deposit box in a bank is a safe way to keep all important papers but the rates are high these days. Therefore buying a home safe is a better thing.

Keeping a notebook of your investments/assets/bank accounts might be simple way for you.

SOME RECOMMENDATIONS FOR YOU:

- Do not skimp on anything that keeps you in good health. Shop in organic food stores and eat healthfully, take vitamins and exercise.
- Have a will in place, living will, put your money in a trust account so your family will have the least amount of problems after your passing. Consult an attorney and get started.....
- Do not skimp on things that bring you a great deal of happiness such as buying a gift for someone you love or taking a vacation, even it is to the next town.
- Long term health insurance: It is costly but necessary. Like any other insurance policy it is a gamble if you will ever need or use it. But if we do need care and we do not have it, we can be wiped out. Nursing is expensive.
- Watch your money and do not put it into the hands of someone else unless if you plan to watch it along with them. Find out about hidden fees when you invest and check your local bank statements monthly as well as checking your telephone and cable bills. Sometimes letters explaining fees are sent in fine small print that we do not bother to read. This goes for other bills, statements that have fine print. We must read and pay attention. Check your mortgage; has it changed? Has your local bank imposed fees you have not noticed? Suddenly my bank started to add on charges that I did not realize at first; one day I caught it and they credited my account. Make sure you check all bills and credit card statements each month.
- Be sure you are not paying fees that you are not aware of. While brokers are around peoples' money all day, they are simply people who can advise you, but it is up to us to make our own decisions and to watch and protect our money always.

- If you have more money than a mate, why not spend it on him?
- Be charitable. When you give you get; the homeless need you. Keep a pocketful of quarters. The first check I write each month is to a charity of my choice.
- Better to live a simpler life and be happy and independent than to be shackled to debt.
- My sister has a motto: If you break or lose something that you love, replace it immediately.

QUESTIONS FOR PERSONAL REFLECTION

1. Is money the root of all evil to you?
2. Does your money talk and bring you empowerment?
3. Do you worry about money or that it might run out? What are you doing now to protect the money that you have?
4. If necessary, can you change your lifestyle? If you are single and alone do you need more than a studio apartment? Blow up beds for guests are wonderful these days.
5. Do you need a car or is it running up your bills?
6. Save and save more; it can't hurt.

*As Elizabeth Taylor once said,
"It is fine to be poor when you are young, but not later in years."*
PROTECT YOUR MONEY AT ALL COSTS.

Notes

Part 4

Enhancing Your Life

29

Education

Watch The Doors Fly Wide Open!

Who remembers the name of your first grade teacher? You do, of course. Who said, "I love going to school?" Who said, "I hate school?" Who longed for those no school days? No matter what, when graduation time came we were in tears, leaving our friends and teachers behind. Our school years were blessed times in all of our lives.

According to Manali Oak, buzzle online 11/24/2011

"Education is important as it teaches us the right behavior and good manners thus making us civilized. Education is instrumental in the development of our values and virtues. Education cultivates us into mature individuals capable of planning for our future and making the right decisions in life. It is education that builds in every individual, the confidence to make decisions, to face life and to accept successes and failures."

It frightened me to raise my hand and to ask questions in class. I thought I would ask the wrong question. My ex-husband once said to me, "Know what I love about you? You sit quietly and let me do the talking." That remark remained in my memory making me fearful to open my mouth, worrying something wrong would come out. It took years for me to raise my hand to get the answers that I needed, and once I started, I never stopped. A simple question can get an answer to be passed on to a child. When one teaches, two learn.

Higher education gives us degrees, while living life teaches us self-knowledge.

Everything in life is a learning experience: relationships, work, a walk in the woods, a class, etc. Being street smart, the ultimate talent, allows us to greet the world with inner common sense. I was present at Lincoln Center's outdoor swing festival, now in it twentieth year. Tonight the son of the Nelson Riddle orchestra is performing and sounding exactly the same as his dad. I never knew Nelson Riddle had a son who is carrying on the beat and the tempo that accompanied the voices of our Ella and Frank. I just learned something new.

There are some people who are blessed with higher intelligence. However, if others do not understand what they are talking about or are made to feel inferior when they speak to you, what is the sense in having a conversation with them? Like any talent a person possesses, a brilliant mind is wonderful to share with the world.

When applying for a job, education and degrees are what employers seek, often even more so than experience. That does not necessarily mean that the person they choose will work out to be the best employee, but in our system, it is the only way to get your foot in the door! However, please ponder this: Suze Orman, the financial wizard brought out some serious points. Students who have taken out a student loan are now finding that they cannot pay back those loans because there are no jobs.

A caller asked, "Do I declare bankruptcy and have my loan erased?"

She answered, "When it comes to the government, you will still be liable to pay it back even if you do declare bankruptcy."

Students wonder if student loans are worth the debt. Perhaps going out and getting a job that does not need a degree is the more sensible way, they reason. Employers may have to change their attitude and go on instinct rather than the perfect résumé. Who wants to be in debt that you cannot repay? What about that student who could have found a cure for cancer, but now has to work as a nurse's aid for fear of not getting a job and being in debt? Scary!

"We are not what we know but what we are willing to learn," says Mary Catherine Bateson (updated on www.marycatherinebateson. com on 8/8/2012).

When it comes to education, we cannot settle for what we already know. I know of two women who will not go near a computer. Both are in their late sixties and aren't willing to go through the frustration of learning something new. They are satisfied with what they already know. Some women only completed high school, some of us went on to higher education but most put their school years to rest. Why stop now? There is much more to learn. Recently I attended a one-day University organized by AARP. It began at 9:00 am and ended at 5:00 p. m. They were clever keeping each class at one hour before boredom had a chance to step in. There were lectures on philosophy, art, architecture, sleep patterns, etc. It was a feel-good day and about 2000 people attended. We all came away with new ideas and inspirations. We had learned something new and spent the day in a great environment.

There are many ways to continue enriching your mind. During the year, community colleges have shorter classes on many subjects. There are concerts and in some cities rehearsal concerts where tickets are inexpensive. If you are a senior there are endless good deals. There is alternative education, night courses, and endless online courses on practically any subject that might pique your curiosity. Google anything you dream of and get answers. One summer I went to real estate school for the heck of it and made a long-term career out of my license. Why not try a course in gardening? Decorating?

Entrepreneurs want to do it their way. Some of us will not make a move into a new vocation without a degree. Taking an ingrained talent you might have and developing it into a business can lead to great happiness and success. All it takes is a good idea and hard work. Don't let age be an excuse. KFC's Colonel Sanders went into business at age seventy-plus. Now many new careers begin at seventy plus, including mine.

Reading is key to learning and now the way we read has changed. We all love our local bookstores but the large chains knocked many out of business. Now the large chains are failing. Will bookstores become obsolete? What does this mean for learning?

Does the Internet take up too much of our time, leaving less time to read? Libraries are in trouble. The beautiful buildings they house are a treasure; a secure place that transforms an ordinary day to one that might bring new enlightenment. There is nothing like holding a book in hand or opening a new book to read. What is a more beautiful sight than seeing a person at peace sitting on a park bench reading? Can that be compared to television or wearing your eyes out on the computer? E-books are the way to go for many readers and digital sales are growing by leaps and bounds. Now we have a choice: paperback or e-book!

SOME RECOMMENDATIONS FOR YOU

- Order a newspaper subscription delivered at your door.
- Become further educated on a subject that interests you. Learn about it online or by ordering a new book, visiting your library, or taking a course. See where it can lead you.
- Ask questions. There are no questions that are not worthwhile.
- Learn a language. Concentrating on the new sound and grammar of a language is one of the best ways to keep your mind alert. A friend of mine studying French is now taking a sabbatical with a French family in Aix De Provence. Here is proof that a new course can swing the doors open to a new adventure.
- Read what you enjoy to read that will enhance your day, no matter what subject.
- Hang out with people who can offer new thoughts and ideas rather than those who enjoy listening to you.

QUESTIONS FOR PERSONAL REFLECTION

1. Do you use your education to inspire others, such as lecturing or mentoring?

2. Would you like to go back to school but think it is too late?

3. Would you like to begin a new project that could bring you happiness and perhaps money but then say, "On second thought, why bother now?" My response is "Please Bother."

4. Do you find yourself bored listening to the same stories of friends over and over, yet there seems nothing new to talk about? Do you lack mental stimulation in your life?

5. Are you a well-educated person always open for new ideas, always inquisitive, loving to learn something new?

6. Some carry around a pocket dictionary. If a word is unfamiliar, they can look it right up. Are you that person?

Education prepares us for the future no matter what stage of life we are in!

Notes

30

Travel

The Best Education

Facebook calculated that I have travelled 42,500 miles, visited 43 countries and have seen 30% of the world. What surprised me more than anything was the extent of miles traveled and what surprised me even more was that I've only seen 30% of the world.

As much as we like to think ourselves well-traveled, some of us boasting that we have been all over the world, none of us can see the whole world in one lifetime. When I ventured out on my first trip to Greece many years ago, I met a fisherman. He told me he has been sailing the Greek Islands for twelve years and he still has not seen all of them. At that moment I realized that I would not either and would have to pick and choose my lifetime travels.

HOW I GOT STARTED ON TRAVELING SOLO:

"One might have a sense of wonder, who lives life as I call it, who has the guts to go out and travel, take risks, get sick on other side of the world" (was how I was decribed by a friend).

In 1978 I was about to leave on my first trip. Recently having separated from my husband, my girlfriend and I planned a two-month trip to Europe. It was a huge thing for me to do; I took a leave of absence from my business, dreaming for months beforehand of what it would be like to spend the summer in Europe. Two weeks before we were to leave my friend cancelled, leaving me devastated. I had gone from my parents' home to marriage, never having experienced going anywhere alone, never mind to another country. What was I to do? Few women traveled by themselves. Then I thought about my two new great friends, my mentors. One was a girlfriend who had left her traditional marriage. She had little money from her settlement but somehow managed a plane ticket and headed to Brazil. She would pitch a hammock on a native's front porch and find her way. She traveled to exotic countries, working as she traveled. May I add that today, forty-five years later, at seventy-six, she is still traveling extensively, spending longer periods of time in Mexico and Europe. She has no intentions of stopping anytime soon and if the day ever comes that she will, where she will be is anyone's guess. Then there was Gerhardt my European lover; he had long blonde hair and was fourteen years younger than me. He would leave his belongings in my apartment and travel around the world alone, later returning to my pad. This was not the type of relationship I had experienced before, so I found it challenging and exciting. I was mesmerized by these two people who were in my opinion, free. But me? Was I ready for this? Was I capable? Could I go solo as they did? I had already rented out my Greenwich Village apartment, making it difficult for me not to go on the trip. I made the decision to follow through on my plans!

I would land in London, where my daughter was living at the time, and hang out there before taking the train to Paris. I packed my oversized heavy duffle bags and placed them on wheels, a new contraption that had just hit the market. My young son escorted me to the airport. With my heart pounding, we said goodbye to each other for two months.

My daughter met me at the airport in London and my adventure began. One week later, I was so comfortable in her apartment and fearful of venturing out that she finally had to say to me, "Mom, it is time to go."

I took the train to Paris without having reservations at a hotel. From the start, locking myself into any situation was not what I wanted to do. Reservations meant being in a place on a certain day and that was not how I wanted to travel. Taxis would not be part of my budget travels, so the subway to the Left Bank was where I was headed. Wanting to do everything on my own figuring things out as I went along by taking public transportation would be challenging to me. However, not knowing French created a great obstacle and not knowing which train went in the direction of the Left Bank and then not knowing where to get off, almost had me in tears. I will never forget the Israeli girl who came to my aid. She pointed me in the right direction and told me where to get off. I lugged my heavy bag through the narrow, intertwined streets, not weakening by grabbing a taxi. I finally found my way to a cool looking European Hotel on the Left Bank that was recommended to me, and sure enough they had room. My room had red velvet drapes and a red bedspread. It was on a corner overlooking the street with its own small balcony. It had a tiny elevator with a gate that would bounce me up and down as I entered and exited. I put my things down and went out for a walk, looking for a place to eat. Before I knew it, I was talking to someone. That is what Europe is all about: sitting in cafes, sipping cappuccino and talking to people. This was going to be OK.

Learning about staying in youth hostels instead of hotels sounded great to me. I would meet more travelers, get more ideas, and so I did. Most travelers were going around the world or had been traveling six months to a year plus; I never knew people did these things; didn't they have to work? They all had huge backpacks and all carried a copy of the Lonely Planet travel guide written in different languages. This was my book as well, which became my loving, reliable, informative best friend and bible, always there for me no matter.

The standard conversation at a hostel went like this:

"Hello, where are you from?"

"How long have you been traveling?"

"Where have you been?"

"Where are you going?"

"Where will you be going after that?"

From those conversations I acquired ideas.

By going to the post office and mailing my things back, I began unloading my ridiculous amount of clothes and the possessions that were weighing me down. I found great difficulty in parting with a single shirt, a dress and other belongings. "What if I need it?" I asked myself. I had packed as a vacationer with matching shoes and was about to become a carefree traveler wearing little or no makeup, clean and comfortable clothes and putting vanity on the back burner. Nobody knew me and I loved the feeling of going incognito, not having to live up to anybody's expectations of me. I began to crave complete freedom without baggage. Later, I learned to leave my worn-out clothes in the last place I visited before my flight home, and nothing made me feel greater than knowing I had worn them out.

One day at breakfast a friend mentioned Corsica. It sounded interesting and thought why not go there? I had never heard of the gorgeous French Island, which would later take me straight to Sardinia. Having no itinerary was excellent; I could go anywhere I pleased on the continent of Europe. Getting there was half the fun: train, boat, then the bus. The Corsican bus driver took an unfortunate liking to me. He wanted me to stay on the bus with him and passed my stop. When I finally did get off, he had taken my wheels, leaving me helpless to carry my still heavy bag in my arms. Then Corsica became a dream and it was there that I had my first travel love affair with a handsome Frenchman. Now do you get the picture? My two month trip was extended to four. There were many times during my travels that I thought I would return to a country that I loved and move there for good. Invariably, as my plane touches down on US soil, my dream suddenly vanishes. This was and still is my style, thirty-five years later. What travel gives to me is a sense of freedom that I cannot equal. I love waking up in the morning in a new place, eating their foods and spending a day in their culture. Then the best part comes! When the feeling comes over me to leave, I board the next train or bus and do it again in a new atmosphere. *Countries are similar to boyfriends, you visit, enjoy the view until you don't anymore and leave. –Ada Calhoun freelance NYTimes 9/16/20.*

I still travel with my wheels but now a small pink backpack is placed on them, with a second smaller athletic bag on top. I wear my walking shoes, take one extra pair of dress shoes, and the rest is stuffed with everyday wear and one or two thin better outfits for dress. My travels have taken me for months at a time visiting the six continents: Europe, Africa, Asia, South and North America, and Australia. Maybe next year I will travel to the seventh, Antarctica. Looking back, I enjoyed the freighter boats going from Italy to Spain and then in Tahiti sleeping outdoors on deck with the locals who deliver food and supplies to the islands along the way. I have slept in converted chicken coops, used the outdoors as toilets and visited some of the most primitive toilets one can ever imagine. In Alaska I refused the popular cruise ship and took the Alaska freighter boat up the passage, sleeping alongside hundreds of travelers.

I loved early morning rises in Greece. I'd wake up in a little village and see groups of men going to a cafe, drinking coffee and smoking endlessly. I will never forget running into my own daughter in a square in Malaysia. I knew she was in Bali but had no idea she was traveling, but there she was hanging out in the village square and on top of it sick with the flu!

There were countless times that I did not want to leave home after booking a trip. Why leave my comfort even to see the exquisite world out there? The minute I arrived at the airport I wondered how I had ever thought of not going on a new adventure.

My style is after a month or so on the road, roughing it in hostels, buses and trains feeling unkempt, I treat myself to a four star hotel and spend the day luxuriating. I walk around the room shouting, "I have arrived in heaven." Wonderful things can happen when you put yourself out there.

I earn money by subletting my apartment. Because I travel economically as one would have to for extended trips, I have been known to come home with more money in the bank. Years ago when the US dollar was strong, living in another country was a great way of saving money. Now, I am hopeful to break even which does not seem to happen too often. As for time, I have always worked for myself so had time to travel, but there have been times I had to cancel a trip because of work. When I didn't, it always served me right to lose out on a great real estate deal.

Travel can be heavenly, but of course one must be careful. In Jamaica, I was once picked up on a highway by a car trying to pin drugs on me. Two undercover cops pulled up in a car with guns. What I didn't realize was the Jamaican couple turned me in for bribe money. Of course I was drug-free so the cops had a hard time pinning anything on me. It took twelve hours of intensely frightening questioning, trying desperately to keep myself alert and awake, to set me free. They kept my passport. It's helpful to be on your best behavior in a foreign country, learning once we leave our country we must follow their rules.

Only in the last couple of years have I graduated from hostels. Now needing my own room for comfort, I choose B&Bs or small hotels. I can no longer share with the snorers, late night people, nor am I interested in bonding as I once did, having lived out those great experiences. Now I find myself at a large five-star hotel, (but only for the day) where I swim and relax at the pool. When I arrive in a city, I usually take an open tour bus to orient myself and then I walk around. I still take local buses to the end of the line looking at residential neighborhoods or anywhere else. When I am in another country I do not drive alone or rent a car, preferring public transportation. I also avoid flying once I am there. I see no sense; I am there to see the country, why fly over it? Take a trip by yourself or take your husband, if married, on a new kind of adventure. You can do it.

With all of my travels two places stand out. One was in Key West, Florida where I went for two weeks, reluctantly leaving my work, and ended up staying four months. It was all of life. I shared the trip down with one son, then another son came, I fell madly in love, I got a job, had many friends and a great apartment.

Then there is beloved India. India is all of us. There we find the peace, love, comfort that most of us do not have in our busy lives. I have included here my story on India, where I visited as a gift to myself for my seventy-fifth birthday.

<u>India 2010 at 75 years old</u>

POSTED BY CAROL SUE GERSHMAN AT <u>10:21</u> PM

As I watched one hot sunny afternoon the air conditioned comfy tour bus, filled with white face faces pull away, I wondered why I sat on the dusty, dirty curb waiting for the National rickety bus to barrel down the road to take me to my next stop.

I took my seat at the open window and felt the fresh breeze on my face from the mountainous air and smiled. Across from me sat two wildly gorgeous Hindi gypsy women lavished in vibrant red and purple saris. Their jewels started on their fingers and their bracelets covered both arms right up to their shoulders. They had a large piece of festive cloth that they tied to the seat handles in front of them making a unique crib for their baby. Another son was dressed from the waist up only. Their spouses who paid no attention to them during the almost four hour trip wore white, with red turbans and they were great to look at as well. At the front of the bus was a Muslim woman who was having a bout with an Indian man. Of course I could not understand one word, but she was screaming at the top of her lungs and putting him in his place. I sat mesmerized the entire trip and why I take the local bus.

It has been much the same here in India for the past six weeks. I feel like I have been on a continuous movie set, part of a strange new world. I have not read more than a few page of Gandhi's autobiography as life is far too interesting; so I watch, witness and then I sleep.

They told me not to come. What are you nuts? India alone? At 75? It is different, the sickness, the poverty, the dirt, the filth. At least take an organized tour or at the very least have an itinerary. I listened, but I believed more in myself and how I like to travel.

I have seen all the Temples, Palaces and Forts that I care to see. I have walked the narrow packed cobblestone paths in their town along side of loving cows. I watch them drink out of public water fountains and had flirtations with many. The dogs roam on the other side of me and monkeys jump over head. I played tic tack toe jumping over the cow shit and dog shit and missed twice. The horns beep from the thousands of motor cycles, rickshaws and cars. Here they ask you to please beep and they do till you want to scream from the noise. The merchants are pushy and try everything to lure you into their shops and again you want to scream "get away from me" and I did.

I have met lovely people and have met myself many times. The shopping is beyond fun and must admit I have gone nuts. My favorite kind of day is cash machine, rickshaw, shop. Next day, cash machine, rickshaw, shop. I have never felt more self indulged.

On the whole, the people are lovely and kind and will do anything to help you. One man gave up his desk and phone for 45 minutes while I tried to correct an airline ticket I bought; bad enough to do in the States. They do not smoke, but chew tobacco instead. While the streets are filled with dirt and dust, the people are clean. The weather has been divine. Rain for one hour the entire 6 weeks.

I witnessed the most poverty at the train stations. Children sleeping on the cement, rats running around, beggars and the terribly deformed with beautiful smiling faces. Then a cow wanders in and I shook my head and laughed. Once on the train there were banana peels under my seat, so I called the attendant. He stooped down, looked and stared and had no idea what I wanted him to do. So I slept with banana peels under my bed.

What is so fascinating about India is that each place is different? The Indian people are wildly colorful. I have swam in the Ganges along side of cows, enjoyed the fresh water pools; The Taj Mahal will never let me forget my seventy-fifth birthday and to watch the prayers and their cleansing in the river is amazing.

There seems to be plenty of food and many of the children are well schooled. In the slum areas they are put to work early depending on their parents. One morning I went out to get my wash that I hung on the line only to see across the field a shack with a mother and two babies. I thought to myself, how can live be this divided. I wandered over to meet them and was invited into their shack. There was one cot, and blankets on the cement floors for the children. They cooked outside, I gave them some money and when I said goodbye I crossed the field back into my life of swimming pools, massages, gorgeous room and delicious food. There by the grace of God go I.

India represents all of life and no place does it better than Varanasi. From the sweet infants, to the thousands of children, to the absolutely gorgeous Indian girls and young moms who grow into fat women, to the deformed, the beggars, the pushers, the old and then the burning ghat where 60 dead people a day are put to rest. This is India where life is lived openly each day, every day.

The last week I decided to go to Osho Ashram in Pune, outside of Mumbai. I had heard about it for many years. I had no idea that I was entering a spiritual concentration camp where I would have to abide by their orders. I had to buy a maroon robe, a white robe to be allowed in. I would have to wear the maroon robe all day long until it was time to change into the white robe in the evening. I was not allowed in their gorgeous lavish pool until I bought a maroon bathing suit. If I was one minute late for any program I would not be allowed in. Once inside I could not cough, sneeze, or clear my throat. There were guards all over checking my ID. I had to take an aids test and after paying their entrance fee, I had to pay to swim in their marble pool. It all gave me a headache and stressed me out; once they tamed the tiger, I did not want to leave.

I would say, if you have not been, hurry up and go. India is growing rapidly and change is, and will be coming fast. Some places are already somewhat westernized; some are caught between at this point. Already they are tourist friendly and tourist ready. This will be the place we are all looking for!

I've been traveling solo for thirty-five years. At the end of each trip I write a travelogue and email it to my family and friends. I do this for two reasons. First, I enjoy taking notes along the way. However, the real reason is this: when I call my family and friends to say I am back, I don't have to repeat the same story. Each one has read about my trip and it then becomes a fun thing to discuss.

SOLO YOU:

What is your style of traveling? If you have not traveled alone yet, would you consider going by yourself? If so, my suggestion is starting with a cruise; that is, if you are not prone to seasickness. The process is simple:

- A flight will take you to the airport.
- The travel agent will pick you up at the airport and deliver you to the boat.
- The porters will take your luggage and you will be given your room.
- Your luggage will not be delivered until later, so all there is to do is go up to the deck and have lunch.

- After lunch walk around the ship and acquaint yourself with the layout. Visit their fabulous gyms and see what they have to offer. Perhaps you will sign up for a facial or a massage.
- Back in your room, rest, turn on the ship's TV and hear what is going on.
- Then with your luggage delivered to your room, dress for dinner. In the dining room you will be given a table where you will meet 6-10 new people.
- Now you are set—maybe! If you do not like your table, ask the maitre' d to sit you at another table.
- For a single woman: ask to be seated with men. On my last cruise I was escorted to a table of two women. Before sitting down I did an about face, going to the maitre' d and requesting a mixed table of both men and women. He did much better by seating me at a table of four men. Men, I learned, cruise and they cruise alone. One was on his fiftieth cruise. They find the best of deals and off they go. All were retired, ranging in age from 56 to 70.
- You might enjoy joining a tour from your ship at one of the cruise ports or taking yourself to the best hotel in town for several hours.
- After having a wonderful time on board, you will pack your things, the porter will take them for you, a taxi will take you to the airport and home you go.

Cruises can be expensive, but it you can afford it and fearful of traveling alone, they are a good way to start.

Once you have cruising under your belt, choose a country that you would like to visit. Book a room from home, but for no more than two nights. If it works out, stay longer, if they don't have a room, I guarantee you will find a better place on your own. Don't lock yourself in to a situation where you have paid up front and are miserable. I prefer to stay in a populated area in walking distance to everything. Walk up and down the street and go room shopping, another part of real estate. Remember to travel light at all costs, travel with bags that do not have to be checked and that you can handle yourself. Shop if you need things; it is such fun to do in a foreign country.

Last year my two sons took me to Prague and Budapest. I had one small black bag and my pink backpack on wheels. In them I had two dressy outfits, and at least five dressy changes, as the plan was to wine and dine me. They both came loaded down with a large suitcase, having porters carrying them as I walked alongside pulling mine.

AARP magazine featured a woman who is eighty-two who backpacks seven to nine months a year going the hostel route. There is a world of travelers out there and now of course a world of women traveling solo.

Use a money belt instead of a bag and please do not forget one comfortable pair of shoes. Find local restaurants to dine; bring a guidebook and read through it beforehand to get ideas. Try not to stay in only one place. Be a traveler rather than a tourist. If you can swing three weeks at the least, which I recommend, stay three nights and travel the fourth to a new place. After a while your trips might become longer; you will want to see more and you might even get bit by the solo travel bug. I love getting on a bus in a foreign land and passing the landscape. Try not to be afraid of not meeting people. It could be a great lesson, as it will give you a chance to go inward. You might discover how you are adapting to new situations, both good and bad, growing from the experience and learning new things about yourself, which is the ultimate discovery. If luxury is your style, stay in a luxury hotel. However, one of the dullest places to stay if you are traveling alone is at a five star hotel unless the room and lobby is more important to you than anything else. It is usually harder to meet people in a large hotel as most people will be coupled, on business or not interested in meeting you. You will have more fun at a hostel or a smaller inn. I do however love to lounge at their pools or treat myself to an elegant buffet breakfast.

Of course there are always tours, a good way to travel even though I am not a fan except for day trips. To me, tours are confining and like they say, On the bus, off the bus, with little adventure and lots to put up with but still beats staying at home any day.

If money is an issue and keeping you back from traveling, aside from paying your airline ticket, you can actually live very cheaply in some countries. If you have saved up enough frequent flier points you might have a free ticket. You can shop in local food markets just as you do at home and prepare your own food in hostels where lodging is inexpensive. Living like you would at home, but away. Some people go to another country and teach English, earning as they go along. You can cut costs by traveling with a friend, but you might not meet others as easily or have the freedom of Only You.

Another way to begin traveling on your own is to take a day trip and see how you fare. Take a bus or train to a destination two hours away from your own home, and perhaps you will extend to an overnight. Stay at a Holiday Inn or such in another town and lounge in the room all day, exercise, take yourself out for dinner. My sister travels extensively, mostly solo, loving her cruises. Then, she will visit different countries, sometimes renting an apartment and staying for a month's time. There are also home exchanges. I prefer hotels, often saying I could live in a hotel room indefinitely. Preferring to move around, I am fearful taking chances of being locked into a situation in somebody's apartment especially for a month; with a hotel, again, I have complete freedom.

My travels in the US take me up and down the highway to Florida on business. I adore hitting the road alone in my car; I find nothing more relaxing than a day on the road, driving six to eight hours a day, checking into a "Choice Hotels" where I gather points. I love ordering in a naughty pizza and resting with television. Then getting up early and doing it all again. Sometimes I wish the trip would never end.

Leaving home is not usually an easy thing to do especially if you sublet your apartment. I have to prepare for my guest by moving closets, cleaning drawers, paying bills to be mailed two months in advance. Begin early to prepare for a trip. Do not leave things for the last two days. About two weeks before a trip, I begin to take my closet apart, putting things aside to take on my trip. Then I have a base to add or eliminate until the last day when I pack.

Please get to your destination early, so there is no panic along the route. Airports can be fun to hang out, eating, reading and much more fun than begging to be let on the plane.

Finally, if you think you are well acquainted with a spot of this planet, go back and you probably will not recognize it, that is why the only place we will ever truly know is home.

SOME RECOMMENDATIONS FOR YOU

- Get a passport. Did you know that only 30% of Americans have one? Many Americans do not leave their own zip code.
- Look at the globe or look into the back of your mind. If there is somewhere to go that you have dreamed about seeing, try your hardest to get there leaving no room for regrets.
- Never give up a trip, or for that matter an evening out, if a friend cancels. Go by yourself. If you feel awkward, I understand, but you will soon get over it. People are not looking at you. They are all too absorbed in their own lives.
- Make sure you are healthy before you leave on a trip. Make copies of all of your documents. Leave one copy with a friend at home and put the second copy in an alternate case you are carrying. It is extremely important that your medical care covers you out of the country. If it doesn't, take out a policy that will cover you and be sure to always have the necessary shots.

QUESTIONS FOR SELF REFLECTION

1. Has this chapter opened any new thoughts or ideas for you?
2. What places would you like to visit?
3. Have you gone alone on a trip and had a terrible time? Why?
4. What kind of a roommate do you make?
5. Is the thought of going alone not interest you at all? Why?

Living a passionate life
includes travel,
the best way to achieve
freedom within
is to travel.

Notes

31

Decorating

Enhance Your Wonderful World!

Oprah asked, "Why do we love decorating so much?"
Recently, I set up a friend's apartment. He moved from a five-bedroom home to a one-bedroom NYC apartment. I met with the movers, unpacked alongside them, and by the second day everything was in place with flowers in the vase. Friends thought that this was very admirable. Are you kidding? It was a delight! Each item I took out of the box was fun to look at and then happily placed around the room. I was decorating!

It is extremely important to like where you live. The outside world can be cold, noisy, harsh. Your home needs to be orderly, comfortable, peaceful and pretty. It is yours to enjoy; to shower, cook, relax and have privacy. Our home reflects who we are and much can be learned about a person when you visit their home; Are you colorful, bland, modern, traditional? Does your home match who you are? Is your bathroom and kitchen clean, is there a certain amount of food in the refrigerator? Do you use tissues as well as toilet paper or toilet paper for tissues? Is your taste expensive or do you live minimally? Our homes tell a great story about us.

Anyone, regardless of income, can have a nice home. I have visited homes in Africa and India. They have cement floors, a cot or a mattress on the floor, but the homes were always neat and clean. The women take pride in where they live and were eager to show me their interior.

So let's decorate:

I first learned about decorating from my mom at age eleven. One summer she surprised me with a beautifully decorated room. She was most proud of the border that she herself put around the ceiling. It had pink flowers on it and there was a matching bedspread. My own decorating began when I was first married. We lived in a little cottage in Wichita Falls, Texas. I moved the furnished sofa to another position in the room, placed an end table putting objects and books on it. It was an adorable cozy little sitting area that we loved. Each stage of marriage brought on increasing rooms to decorate. I wondered why my friends used a decorator; it was so much more fun to do it myself.

Once I slip covered my whole apartment in red, white, and blue silk using hat pins. It was a temporary sublet; the walls were bland and I could not spend the next six months living in a dreary setting. I went to my storage garage, (I was in the party design business) and brought home props. I hung large cutouts of giant elephants on the wall, bought a superman spread and turned my brownstone studio into a circus room with balloons, down to the peanuts in a bowl. It was too much fun. I thought it was so great that I had the interior designer of Bloomingdale's come over as I thought it would make a great July 4 window in their store. He got a big kick out if it, especially liked my slip covers, but it did not make it into their window. My son came home from college and brought a friend with him to visit his mom. They walked in with a gasp; they will forever talk about that day. Decorating can be a great creative outlet and something you can do repeatedly.

Take a good look around your home. Do you like what you see? Keep it simple. There is creativity in all of us. Yes, mistakes are costly but the more you decorate, the more experienced you become. Set aside a certain amount of money and try to stay within the budget. Understand, it invariably costs more than budgeted, but there are many ways to save, especially if you are willing to do certain things yourself.

- A simple coat of paint and rearranging your furniture within the same room can turn your old room into new. Move pieces around and you will be surprised.
- While eloquent pieces of furniture are a gem, I prefer the furniture I pick up on the street and re-do; I transformed a lounge chair thrown into the garbage with a coat of pink paint and a new cushion. To me that is fine furniture.
- Going to thrift shops or garage sales is surely a great way to get something at a great price. Unfortunately kitchens and bathrooms get more expensive, unless of course you are married or have a friend who is a plumber.
- I wanted pure white carpeting under my bed. Instead of tearing the old flat surfaced carpet up, I decided to paint it. It came out beautifully and it is easy to maintain. It is easily cleaned with Oxiclean or I just take out my paints. Do not try in on a shag; it has to be a tight woven flat material and it does take buckets of paint on the first round, but beats new installation.
- Add greenery; plants give our homes a wonderful feeling. Nothing is gospel. If you want your living room to look like a beach or a garden, why not do it? Beach furniture and hammocks in a living room are fun. Use a picnic

table in the dining room made to look like an outdoor patio. The more creative you are the better you will feel.

- Buy material and cover old pillows. If you do not like to sew, tie the material in a thin knot or pin it.
- My art is my family photos. I have a large wall covered with plastic box frames housing wonderful colorful photos of family. I find it interesting to see how many guests enjoy them and it is even more interesting to see how many guests don't enjoy them.
- Go easy on fake flowers or plants. One lovely vase of fake flowers is fine, but don't put them all over your home.
- Some people like to spray their home with scents. It can be offensive. There is nothing like a pot of apples with cinnamon boiling on your stove.
- In small spaces, keep it light and airy rather than filling it with heavy pieces or dark colors. In larger areas you can have larger pieces and deeper colors.
- Make your bed something special. A painted headboard, or up against a wall with pillows, or a painting; anything at all goes. Thrift shops can offer linens as well as a great coverlet and don't forget about a canopy bed, men love them too.
- Recently I ordered white sheer drapes. They came in too long, so I got out a needle and thread and put a stitch one foot apart at the hem making the bottom of the sheers puff.
- Old drapes can be made fresh by adding a panel of a different color, something you can pin on the drape from the top at intervals in a soft flowing material about one foot apart. Buy remnant material and hem all around. Let the extra piece flow freely.
- If you have an old beat up wood floor, paint it, rather than refinishing it. I have discovered great paint for this. It is outdoor sign paint and it covers like no other. I used the same white paint on my old kitchen cabinets and they look new.

- Never be afraid to mix your fabric patterns: polka dots, plaids, and same goes for furniture. Modern, contemporary, traditional all in one room mixed and matched is more interesting.
- Put something sweet that is inexpensive such as a vase, a tray, an ornament that you like on a table.
- Try adding a drop of red to a room decorated in other colors. Your eye will be drawn to that one red thing.
- Don't be afraid to use color; there is nothing like it.
- I have used several night tables put together to form a dresser. It gave me more drawer space.
- Our decorating eye, our creative eye is constantly changing with new thoughts and ideas.
- A great place to pick up things for your home is when you travel and probably one of the best places to shop is at the airport as you leave.
- A great way to start your project is to collect pictures and articles and put them into a special folder. Go to a paint store and bring home samples of paint colors and start scotch taping them on walls. Begin with a color scheme. Some people believe that buying a rug first is the best way to decorate, sometimes adding a rug is also the best way.
- Often we don't even realize that our interior spaces can govern our mood, our outlook on life, even how happy we are to be alive. Doctors' offices, schools, large institutions, banks, need design and of course the stores where we shop. It is essential that restaurants are clean and have an inviting decor which can cost millions. Therefore we live in a decorated world. Anything that has an interior can be designed, redesigned or refurbished.

SOME RECOMMENDATIONS FOR YOU

- Do not clutter. Get rid of pieces that take away a rooms freedom. Use three or four comfortable chairs around a coffee table instead of a large sofa.
- Collect your ideas before pouncing and don't forget to measure.
- Shop and compare. Furniture, linens, lamps. Items are expensive. Get the right value by shopping online. It will be your home for a long time.
- Shop in stores where they will allow returns especially on large items, such as rugs, furniture.
- Think about lighting. Put all the lights you can on dimmers to give you control of the atmosphere.

QUESTIONS FOR PERSONAL REFLECTION

1. Do you enjoy decorating?
2. Are you afraid of making a costly mistake so to avoid that, you hire a decorator?
3. Have you tried to decorate but it did not come out as you had hoped?
4. Do you feel you lack creative ability?
5. Do you choose having a decorator because it has been the social climbing thing to do?
6. Would you think of trying a small corner of your room to see how it could be enhanced by only your taste?

Now take another look around. It seems we are never finished decorating.

32

Clutter

Shopping For Something New Today?

"Three Rules of Work: Out of clutter find simplicity; From discord find harmony; In the middle of difficulty lies opportunity."
- Albert Einstein

Isn't it true that when you clean out a closet or a drawer it makes you feel good? We have all created our own clutter by simply bringing increasingly more things into our home and minds. There is nothing as welcoming as an orderly space. Yet we shop for things and in the end giving up those things is not an easy thing to do.

Here are some great declutter tips including those from *Babuata, Zen Habits Breathe 1/24/2007.*

1. De-clutter for 15 minutes every day. Look around and remove. Start at the corner by the door and move your

way around the room. Don't allow things into the house. Focus on what you are buying and if you really need it.

2. Donate stuff you're de-cluttering or place out on the street. Before your very eyes it is gone.

3. Whenever you're boiling the kettle for tea, tidy up the kitchen. This is a wonderful tip as much gets accomplished till the teakettle whistles. Use the "one in, two out" rule. This is a hard one as it is about letting go.

4. Make your storage space smaller and more minimal. If you have storage, you'll fill it with stuff. My storage space in my basement runneth over. If you are fortunate enough to have good storage space put things away carefully as your storage room can become even worse than the room you are de-cluttering.

5. Clothing rule: If you haven't worn an item in six months, sell or donate it. The fewer the things I have in my closet the happier I am. It is much easier to select what to wear and what goes with what. Another wise idea is to rotate your closet, putting things at the back and bringing them back up front in several months. Now they seem new. I have two closets, one for my wardrobe, the other for coats, jackets amongst the vacuums. A closet packed tightly that the contents fall down when you open the door makes life more difficult.

6. Hide your dressy shoes and keep three pairs of shoes in sight. If you live in a small space, it is imperative to keep de-cluttering your possessions all the time.

7. The One-Year Box. Take all your items that you unsure about getting rid of e.g. "I might need this someday." Put them in a box, seal it and date it for a year in the future. When the date comes, and you still didn't need to open it to get anything, donate the box.

8. De-clutter one room (including any closets, desks, cabinets, etc.) before starting on the next one. Spending

time in that room will feel so good, and it will be so easy to keep clean, that it will motivate you to do more! I keep a tray on my desk where I place mail and papers that I go through every few days. How many of us clutter our desks. Why 12 pens? How about one good one that we cherish. Keep your papers organized but don't use too many folders as they tend to get cluttered with papers you cannot find. Keep an incoming and outgoing folder. I place all of my monthly bills in a small gift bag that is colorful and I add to that bag until the month is up. I keep a separate small gift bag for envelopes, stamps and return stamps. These are neatly placed in a drawer.

9. Keep a list in your planner labeled "Don't Need It – Don't Want It." When you're out shopping and run across some kind of gadget or other item you crave, note it down on the list. This will slow you down long enough to reconsider. Also, seeing the other things on the list that you nearly bought on impulse really helps.

10. Gift everything. Books you've read immediately get recycled among friends, family or local libraries. If you buy a new gaming system, donate your old one – and all the games.

SOME RECOMMENDATIONS FOR YOU:

- Tiny women often carry around huge heavy bags. When we clutter our purse and wallets there is more to lose or more for someone to steal. It is a lovely feeling to walk out with nothing or a tiny bag. It is best to keep one credit card and one bank card, a driver's license and in cities, a transportation card.

- Keep your fridge clutter-free. Europeans shop every day. We tend to join Costco, Sam's Club, buying in huge amounts. Unless if you are a large family, why do that? Once a month buy the necessary oil, vinegar and mustard and then shop twice a week.

237

- There is nothing nicer than stepping into someone's clean and neat car, especially your own, one that does not smell from cigarettes, where the mats are clean and there is room to sit without cat/dog smells. Obviously I have been in those environments. Cars tend to get filled with stuff.
- Try to live with bare walls or one lovely piece you enjoy.
- I've always made photo albums. I have tons of albums and hardly a place to keep them. It is best not to be an avid collector. I wonder what my children are supposed to do with all of these photos, but I dare not part with them during my lifetime, storing them in closets, in ottomans, in storage rooms keeping some exposed.

- For most of us, we clutter our homes by bringing in too much stuff and not being able to part with it. Once you learn how to give things away to charity or run a garage sale, you will feel free and want to give away more and more until it becomes second nature. Here is another point of view:

  I believe one of the best definitions of clutter comes from Karen Kingston's book *Clear Your Clutter With Feng Shui*. Here are her four categories of clutter:
  • Things you do not use or love
  • Things that are untidy or disorganized
  • Too many things in too small a place
  • Anything unfinished

  These categories help us define for ourselves what is cluttering our own home.

- I prefer this over other people telling me something is clutter and I should get rid of it, when for me it isn't clutter. For example, most people would say that old magazines are clutter. Makes sense, except I have collected many issues of a particular decorating magazine that I love and regularly peruse repeatedly because I find doing so is peaceful to me. Old issues of this magazine also often sell for three times or more the regular cover price on eBay. I use and love this magazine; therefore it's not clutter. However, I recently tossed out many other old magazines I've collected because I wasn't using them and didn't love them.

- When defining whether your own stuff is clutter simply ask yourself if it fits into one of these four categories. Also ask yourself: Do I still like this outfit, use this, does it fit, is it still me?

QUESTIONS FOR PERSONAL REFLECTION

1. Do you have tips on how you de-clutter?
2. Does parting with a possession inhibit you moving somewhere new because you cannot part with your things? Perhaps as simple as, "What would I do with my dining room table? I can never live without it, therefore I will not move." Don't get stuck with your possessions!
4. Do you live in a home that is overwhelming with stuff? Have you gotten used to it? Take a good look around your home and see if what you see pleases you. Will you make a commitment to improving your home by getting rid of things?
5. Are you a person who has other interests and who pays no attention to how you live thinking who cares, what does it matter? Have you asked yourself, Why you own a certain piece, what could you get rid of and never miss, why you need it and what is it costing you to own it?

33

Fun and Games and Sports

When Was The Last Time You Kicked A Football?

L ife is better when you know how to play a game or do a
sport, as it will open other doors.

Do you play cards, Mah Jongg, Scrabble, Bridge,
Monopoly, poker? A game shared with other people is a terrific
way to socialize as well as the utter enjoyment of the game.

My game is Mah Jongg. It is a Chinese game that Jewish
women have adopted. In fact, I realize that Jewish people not
only love Mah Jongg, we love Chinese food as well.

Games seem to form a social friendship, a special bound
for the love of the game. If all else fails, when I arrive at my
Mah Jongg game, I am happy and eager to play; and so are my
playmates. We share our life experiences, wealth, health, love,
recipes, friends, problems but once we begin to play, we can
think of nothing else than winning the hand. My friend wrote
a new play called "Mah Jongg," the musical based on what goes

on at the Mah Jongg table. Women are women and the gossip is terrific!

When I was in my twenties raising kids it was rewarding to take a break from the kids and play Mah Jongg. My husband did not appreciate it as he watched his mother play and it identified me too closely with his mother. I found myself lying to my husband as I snuck out to play!

After my separation I didn't play for thirty-five years. Then one day, only seven years ago it reentered my system. What was equally strange is that many who gave it up back then, also began to crave the game; We are back in full force!

The fun can grow by putting money into a kitty and planning a trip or celebration. This can happen with any group activity.

Sports are fun too. Tennis anybody? Soccer? Join the crowd and watch. Here come the Olympics. Going to a Knick's game in NYC is a 100% New York experience; the crowd roars and boos. Going to the stadiums of the world to enjoy baseball and football games is a national pastime. Horseracing and the Super Bowl make history every year. Even if you are not a sports lover it makes great conversation.

We can do almost anything on a computer: watch movies, play games, Google topics of interest and it keeps growing beyond our imagination. Meet me on Facebook; I am there and love it; to me it's just fun. Computers are wonderful for seniors and for young children. My first computer was a Dell and I wanted to take it and throw it out of the window never thinking I could learn. Going to computer school was even more complicated. When I think back it was only seven years ago and now I am almost embarrassed to admit I am always on the computer. I suggest a Mac computer as once you learn it, it is easy. I have not experienced the same crashes and frustrations that my Dell caused me. It knocks out the computer people in

India who truly can give you a nervous breakdown when you need internet support. One almost did. What about learning a musical instrument?

QUESTIONS FOR PERSONAL REFLECTION

1. Is there a game you once knew that you would like to start again?
2. Every town has meet up groups on internet. I found a dear friend on a meetup group site under Mah Jongg players. Go to the internet to find friends who enjoy what you do. This new world is at our fingertips. Will you give it a shot?
3. Does your husband/wife enjoy playing board/card games with you? Couples games are a terrific idea.

The true character of people comes out over the card table or how high they can kick that football.

Notes

34

Home Entertaining

How Gracious Are You?

I have a friend who lives alone but each night she sets her table with a lovely setting and sits down to dinner. She enjoys a beautiful centerpiece as well. That is a lovely thing to do for yourself if you live alone. Single women tend to do everything in their bedrooms, including eating. A beautiful set tray in bed is another thought. Entertaining is a wonderful thing to do for yourself and others. While being a guest is lovely, entertaining guests is far more creative. Each Sunday my family invited our relatives to our house where my grandmother would cook, my mom and I would serve and later do the dishes. Mind you, this is after they worked six days a week. It bonded all of us. At our recent cousins club meeting the topic of conversation was the wonderful dinners we shared.

Entertaining became a big part of my life carrying on the tradition of my family. At our home, there were countless dinner parties, backyard Coney Island parties, pool parties, ending up with the biggest splash of all, our son's Bar Mitzvah. The idea for my son's Bar Mitzvah came to me in the middle of the night. I shot up in bed, awakened my husband, saying, "I got it, I got it! I will tent the entire backyard and the swimming pool will look like a pond in the middle of the tent. Our guests will be seated at tables and chairs around the pool." I was out of my mind with excitement in the middle of that night, my husband pissed that I would wake him over such a thing. While the competition was fierce amongst Bar Mitzvah parties, all trying to make theirs the best, ours was simply gorgeous. Nature did her part by giving us a bright sun shining day allowing the sun to gleam through the huge yellow and white tent shining over the turquoise pool. It was so successful that a friend said, "You should do this professionally." That started Party Artistry, a party design business. Designing weddings, bar mitzvahs, and charity balls became my career for more than ten years until I sold it to my sister who is still carrying on after forty years with her daughter, my neice. If you follow your talents and keep an open mind, life will present you with unimaginable opportunities.

Home entertaining can be simple. There is no such thing as not enough space as people prefer to gather in small spaces. Certainly a room has to have good ventilation and room to walk around, but gathering together ends up to be more enjoyable. Even if you have a large home, it is best not to sprawl your guests over a large area.

Recently we were invited to a friend's home for the weekend. She invited four women to play Mah Jongg in her lovely home in upstate New York. She chose to sleep in her finished basement, giving everybody our own private room. Each morning, noon and night she served lavish meals around her dining room table. There was salmon for lunch and filet mignon for dinner. Nobody had more fun than she did. Her remark was, "I don't care if you take only one bite and nothing more; I loved the preparation and the fun I had cooking." We all walked away with the most wonderful feelings from this marvelous host.

Some of us feel the same as she did, loving to cook and prepare and serve. It is an art that receives instant satisfaction hearing the oohs and ahhhs from guests.

For the past twenty years my sister has entertained her family and friends at her annual Thanksgiving Day dinner. What she does is extremely unique! When the guests arrive, appetizers and drinks are awaiting us in her living room with the furniture in place. Since she is in the party business, the tables are lavishly set and placed in the corners of the room while we are having appetizers. Each year she surprises us with a different theme. After cocktails, we are asked to leave the living room and go into her bedroom while the men are summoned to take the living room furniture out of the living room and place in the hallway replacing it with the already set tables. The chairs are whisked into place, the guests seated, the buffet ready under two beautiful crystal chandeliers. Bravo!

Here are some helpful tips on the art of entertaining:

- Don't leave anything for the last minute. Plan and design your party and food well in advance so that you are not a nervous host.
- Choose a menu that does not keep you at the stove. Freeze ahead and if possible hire someone to pop things in and out of the oven. If you have hired a caterer be sure that you have sampled the menu to your taste. These days it is not as easy as before to please everyone. *There are those who are gluten free, dairy free, vegan, low fat, low sodium, no carbs, no dairy, soy-less, meatless, wheat-less, macrobiotic, probiotic, antioxidant, says Jessica Bruder a New York Times writer. However, if you stick to foods all people like such as salads, potatoes, vegetables and a meat and a pasta dish, it should all turn out well.*

- Make your guests feel at home making sure that you remember their names so they can be properly introduced. Practice this beforehand if you are not that familiar with some of your guests.
- Start the conversation by mentioning what one person does or is going to do, compliment, and quietly slip away to meet others leaving other folks to talk amongst themselves.
- Make your guests comfortable. They come first and nothing should be too much for you to insure that they do. While people like to stand when sipping a cocktail, have a few chairs around for those who like to sit. Take out large pieces of furniture if space is needed.
- While a clean house is necessary, it is best to do heavy cleaning after the party.
- Food and drinks should be plentiful. This is not a time to skimp. For early arrivals greet them with a drink and something to eat. No need to wait for all to arrive. A small amount of leftovers will insure that you had plenty of food.
- Have background music playing softly and as the evening goes on, the music can be turned up. Keep the room dimly lit. Lighting is everything, lower the lights for a soothing evening.
- Temperature is important. Some like it hot, some cold. I will never forget going to a friend's wedding. She was always hot, so she put the temperature below freezing. We sat and froze trying to cover up our beautiful new dresses while she enjoyed how she felt. In summer, have air conditioning and fans and try to be considerate to all needs, not saying it is easy.
- When you are serving wine, cocktails, have plenty of bottled water, Perrier for those who do not drink. Nonalcoholic beer is wonderful.
- Don't disappear for long stretches into the kitchen. The host needs to be present making sure the conversation

is flowing, the music perfect and if it is catered, that the caterers are serving at the right time.

- Make sure there is adequate parking. If not, hire a valet or arrange car pools for people who live near one another, so instead of three cars there is one. If you are having a large party notify your neighbors and the police for those party poppers that call to end your party.

- Please do not over react if someone spills a drink or breaks a glass. Get something to clean up the mess quickly handling their embarrassment. Everything can be cleaned or replaced. However, how you handled the situation will long be remembered. If there is something that is precious to you, remove it for the party even if it enhances your ambiance.

- Please do not turn away a guest if someone arrives with a person who has not been invited. Greet them well and set a place for them, even if it means giving up your own. Your guest may not have done the right thing, but you did.

Marni Jameson is a humorous syndicated home-design columnist, speaker, and author of *House of Havoc* and *The House Always Wins*. Here are her thoughts:

- Give guests something to do. When guests arrive to a party, no matter how confident they are, they have a sense of trepidation, said Matheson. Give them a task. Point them to the self-serve bar, or the appetizers. "Handing someone a drink as they walk in deprives them of the opportunity to walk through the room, and get a drink and their bearings," she said.

- Be sincere. Paying compliments is one of the nicest ways to make others feel good. However, Matheson notes the two kinds of compliments you should never give: False and backhanded. "You must look for something honest, kind and sincere to say. Avoid gratuitous remarks; people can smell a phony. No compliment should carry any tinge of insult. Instead of saying, 'Boy, you sure knocked that baby weight off!' try, 'Wow! You'd never know you just had a baby!'"

- Toast with class. Toasts are not roasts and should never be insulting.
- Let others talk. Don't try to dazzle company with your wit. The best way to make someone comfortable is to listen closely to what they have to say, and to care. "Charm happens when people don't think too much about how they're coming across," Matheson said.
- Above all, don't check your phone. "That's the opposite of charming," Matheson said. Mobile devices have no place at a party, or any time you're face-to-face with people you care about.

Make your life entertaining by entertaining yourself or others. If you are alone on your birthday choose a restaurant and invite others to celebrate dutch treat. Tell them not to bring gifts, just come and celebrate your day. Surprise them with a great birthday cake or drink. I thought it was not a proper thing to do until I realized people do not care. Everybody likes to get together and nobody really cares about paying for their own lunch/dinner. The Birthday girl will have a wonderful day of friends rather than sitting home alone.

QUESTIONS FOR SELF REFLECTION

1. When was the last time you entertained? Did you enjoy it? If so, how soon will you plan something else?

2. Are you a better guest than a host? Some people truly are. You might be the guest everybody wants at their party. Yet, entertaining others has never been your forte.

3. Do you lack friends to invite to your home? If so, try to cultivate interests that will bring you to meet new people.

4. What was the greatest party you ever had? Why was it that good?

5. Can you add some more tricks to being a great host?

Share your home, your food and your wine with those who are gracious enough to receive it.

Notes

35

How To Be A Great Guest:

Start With "Thank You For Inviting Me."

Be kind and appreciative of your invitation. First, let your host know when you will be arriving and even more important, when you will be leaving. This should not be a guessing game or see how it goes game.

If you are coming for an overnight or more arrive with a gift. Food is a wonderful thing to bring when you'll be staying overnight. Bring a speciality item from your hometown: breads, cheeses, sweets, fruits, wine, champagne or chocolates. If your invite is not clear tell your host that you would like to go grocery shopping with them. If they decline, you have made the gesture and still nice for you to pick up some loose items.

Some prefer to send a gift afterwards after seeing what the host needs, but still walk in with something small even if you plan on the latter. Be considerate. It is not a good idea to bring flowers or a gift to be used that evening as it could be a nuisance.

Send flowers early in the day or come prepared with your own vase so you can take care of the placement in the vase. It could become a chore for the host.

If they have made and served you dinner, taking them out the next day is a gesture that would be appreciated. Going out for a yummy breakfast always starts the day off great.

Try to help with chores and especially keep your own things neat and out of sight. No matter how gracious the host might be, they would prefer to see their home look the same as before you arrived. Help with the dishes, yes you are a guest, but be a helpful guest. Your host is not there to serve your every comfort; always ask what you can do or simply do. Some truly don't want help and if that be the case, respect that too.

Please wake up and shower and brush your teeth, wearing a clean robe or clothes. Nobody likes to look at an unkempt smelling person especially in their own home.

Always ask how to leave your bed. Usually stripping your sheets and bringing them down to a washing machine is helpful. Sometimes you can put clean sheets right back on the bed. Make your bed each day and keep the room looking clean and neat. Friends may stop by and your host might want to show your home to other people.

Many years back my husband and I were invited as guest to a magnificent home in South Hampton, NY. We were really looking forward to it but upon arrival the host was sick and had no way to get in touch with us beforehand. We were disappointed and rude enough to stay. If this should happen to you, and if possible, clear out; don't burden a sick person even more.

If you are fortunate enough to have your dog invited, whether it be a dinner party or over night, please don't bring a yapping pet that is not house broken. A quiet dog, or one that is kept in a cage bag is fine if you have been pre screened to bring your pet. Nobody wants to put up with an annoying pet.

If you get up during the night, flush the toilet, but wait to open the door until the sound disappears. Take your things with you out of the bathroom if you are sharing it. Bring in your toothbrush each morning but don't leave it on the sink for the next day.

Try to entertain yourself if your host seems busy. Take a walk, take a drive, ask if anything is needed at the store, go to your room or away from host. As a guest, try to behave independently rather than waiting for your host. Enjoy yourself; go sightseeing, take local buses, take a couple of hours' break especially on longer holidays. Both you and your host will feel refreshed.

Be appreciative that you were invited, remembering always that you are a guest and don't live there. When it comes to visiting your own children, make no mistakes: clean, cook, shop and leave your room spotless. Better yet, stay in a hotel or have them visit you.

Internet can be tricky if you are a person who is often online and do not have your own computer. If necessary, ask your host to get you online and shut you down. Do not open the computer, it could change the settings as I have done exactly that to a friend.

Do not invite friends who might be in the neighborhood unless you have cleared it with your host.

Leave a cute note if you leave after your hosts. When they come home they will enjoy reading it.

HOW TO BE AT YOUR BEST AT A DINNER PARTY

- Again, arrive nicely dressed with a small or large gift in hand. It is best not to bring flowers unless if you are coming with a vase and will do the work. The host has her hands full and finding a vase and cutting the flowers could become a chore.
- Don't complain about the temperature in the room or that the food is not anything you can eat, or the chair is uncomfortable or can you sit next to who if seating has been arranged.
- Be polite, put your napkin on your lap.
- Please don't stand up and grab the food as it is placed in center of table. Wait your turn, pass the plate or wait until it comes to you. Once many years ago I entertained friends for dinner. I cooked all day and invited friends over. No sooner had I set the tray down, my guests stood up and grabbed the food I had so decoratively put on the plate and before I could get to my chair.
- Grin and bear and taste or inform the host before that there are certain foods, dietary restrictions you must follow asking if she can accommodate you.
- At the end of the meal the host is usually tired, so please be considerate by not asking for that extra cup of tea or glass of water unless of course it has been offered.
- Helping to clear the table and being the first one up to do so is usually greatly appreciated; stacking dishes for the dishwasher. You will know immediately if the host does not want help, because she will immediately tell you to sit down. If she does not, you know you are on the right track. Always offer help.
- Dinner party gatherings are meant for an enjoyable evening of good food, wine, and conversation. Be friendly to other guests by smiling and enjoying the other people at the table and trying to reach out to each one especially those that sit mute or are shy.

QUESTIONS FOR SELF REFLECTION

1. As a guest are you all the above, some of the above?
2. Do you reciprocate by inviting the host to your home or another kind gesture?
3. Let us hope you were not a bad guest who was demanding, unkempt and ate all of your hosts food with the attitude, "You invited me so I am here to be waited on, car keys please?" You would be surprised!

Are you a better guest than a host?
That's a good thing to be too.

Notes

36

The Arts

Get Out Your Coloring Book and Crayons

Sometimes when we think of art, we think about a painting. There are many forms of art, from photography to architecture to dance to sculpture to painting and beyond; there is something for everyone. It's important to cultivate a knowledge and appreciation for art.

The best way to learn about art is to visit a museum and spend one to two quality hours. Museums take work to visit. Rather than coming home exhausted and forgetting much of what was viewed, try spending less, rather than more, time on your visit. It is also advisable to decide what you would like to see beforehand, as museums are usually vast with tons to absorb encompassing many floors. It makes for a wonderful educating and interesting time if you do not overdo it making sure you wear comfortable shoes.

Award winning author Paulo Coelho wrote on his website, "Museums give people entertainment. Even if you are not interested in art or history, there is always something to catch your attention. Museums reflect our history, our art, our values, our creations and our dreams. It is an easy way to obtain knowledge."

My all-time favorite, the Museum of Modern Art in New York City, offers an extremely festive atmosphere along with its wonderful exhibits. With their outdoor garden space, where people can relax and converse, and two marvelous movie theaters showing an array of fascinating films, it makes for a brilliant time. They have several restaurants as well. At MOMA one can enjoy lunch, an exhibit and a film.

The Barnes museum in downtown Philadelphia has recently opened against Mr. Barnes wishes of moving his famous collection from the suburbs. "As a result his quirky institution is suddenly on the verge of becoming the prominent and influential national treasure that it has long deserved to be. It is also positioned to make an important contribution to the way we look at and think about art along and has increased the visitors to the city." There is always a museum to explore in or near your home town. Check the Internet and local universities, which often have university collections open to public viewing.

On the other hand, might you want to avoid museums? Paulo Coelho's blog makes an interesting argument for this idea: *This might seem to be absurd advice, but let's just think about it a little: if you are in a foreign city, isn't it far more interesting to go in search of the present than of the past? It's just that people feel obliged to go to museums because they learned as children that traveling was about seeking out that kind of culture. Obviously museums are important, but they require time and objectivity— you need to know what you want to see there, otherwise you will leave with a sense of having seen a few really fundamental things, except that you can't remember what they were.*

There are many nontraditional ways to engage with art these days as well. Art Basel in Miami turns the city into a giant playground of art stretching throughout town with parties and exhibits. It is fabulous for art lovers, dealers and party people who flock in from all over the world to be part of the grand event.

SOME RECOMMENDATIONS FOR YOU

- Children love museums; the wonderful children's museums that have sprung up all over the country are a great way to spend time with a child. An adult watching their child or grandchild at this museum will find pure joy seeing them go from playing Firefighter to Cinderella, making ice cream sundaes as an example, ending with drawing or coloring. What is more memorable to a kid than the planetarium? All of those stars right overhead.
- Becoming a member of your local museum is worthwhile. Not only are you supporting your community, you will be invited to member exhibits, wine tastings and meet interesting people. I belong to three museums and try to visit openings as well as inviting friends to join me for an exhibit.
- Even if you are not a museumgoer, try to visit your local museum at least two times a year.
- When you travel, decide how much of museum life you want to give to your vacation. Botanical gardens are a lovely place to spend time. Recently, the Bronx Botanical Gardens recreated Monet's garden home in France and it is a dream to view the magnificent flowering trees, plants and pathways of flowers. Seeing beauty and being part of a beautiful environment enhances "The Amazing You."
- Ballet dancers dancing on their tippy toes while fluttering their arms, leaping high into the air in

time with the music is probably the most beautiful art form there is. A season subscription is sure to enhance your life. It makes one feel good to get dressed up and place yourself in the environment of people who are sharing with you their love for culture and beauty. Then there are the modern forms of dance.

- Go to a symphony, a lovely way to relax. Often I bring something to read. I enjoy looking up on the stage to the magnificent sounds and lowering my eyes to a great writer. This is art. The opera is remarkable especially if you like tragedy.

- Most women and men at one point of their lives will try art lessons both for fun and to find out if they have talent. Painting can be that of furniture, clothing and any thing you can think that will color your life or others.

- What about theater? There are many Broadway, off-Broadway shows and the magnificent concerts and operas all over the world.

- While live art tickets are expensive, there are many ways to get freebies. One idea is to go at intermission as many leave. Approach them nicely and ask if they are giving up their seat and is it possible to have their ticket. You can also go before a performance. There is usually someone who cannot make it and will be trying to sell their ticket. I have gone to many performances this way. There are senior tickets available in all cities all over the world. There are websites to join such as Free Things to do in your city. For a small fee there are many offerings. There is little excuse to deprive yourself of culture.

- There is also the art of a film seen in some great small art theaters. There are film festivals all over the world giving many young film makers the opportunity to present their films. Wherever you look, there is art from the shoes you are wearing to the furniture you are sitting on.

QUESTIONS FOR SELF REFLECTION

1. Please describe your love of the arts and how you partake.
2. Do you belong to museums or have season tickets to art forms?
3. Have you been lazy not going to museums or enjoying the arts, finding little time to partake?
4. If this has not been an interest of yours, would you think to cultivate it?

Take a look around at all the art that has been created

Notes

37

Grandchildren

They Grow Up Much Too Fast!

Children are entertaining and educational, which is why they are included in this part of book. If you are blessed to have grandchildren, how much do you love to be with them? There are the hands on grandparents, long distance grandparents and the ones who are too busy with their own lives to spend time with their grandchildren. Whoopi Goldberg had a line about grandchildren. She said, "I love you, I love you, I love you…here!" meaning we can hand them right back to their parents.

It is said that grandchildren are the gift we get from having our kids. They are a treat that allows you to go back in time and have the fun you might have missed bringing up your own children. That said, grandparents need to follow the rules laid down by their children. The relationship we have with our grandkids often has much to do with the relationship we had with our own children. How a grandparent deals with her own daughter's grandchildren, opposed to daughter-in-law is sometimes different and the only advice on this subject is to develop a good relationship with your daughter and or son-in-law if you want to be close with your grandkids. Will your own kids allow you to bond with them or are your kids worried that you might instill some idea without their approval based on how you brought them up?

I apologized for reprimanding my granddaughter. My daughter-in-law said, "Please don't be sorry, I need your help." I felt wonderful. Are you able to bond and feel free to teach them or discipline or do you need to ask permission to act otherwise?

No matter what, keep in mind how important it is for a grandchild to have a grandparent. We are a gift to them as well that goes straight into their memory. They may take advice from you that they would never take from their own parents. We are of another generation, we can see things differently at times, we have been through it.

I am sorry to say, with divorces, chances are grandparents might have been bad mouthed by their daughter or son-in-law. When your grandchild hears their grandparents talked about, it takes much for them to overcome until they are old enough to understand the true situation. I wish that couples would understand the importance of leaving parents out of the anger and sometimes hatred in the presence of their kids.

It is important to remember them on birthdays, send Valentine's cards and little special gifts that they can remember.

Fun changes as the kids get older. When they are little going to the zoo, swimming, activities, playgrounds were great. As they grow, they might like to shop, go to movies. I once took my seven-year-old granddaughter out on a dinner date. I had a vision of both of us getting all dressed up and going to a fancy trendy restaurant. We did get dressed, we did go to the restaurant, we did have a great table, but she was so tired waiting for our fancy dinner to be served that she fell asleep at the table. We can't rush things.

One grandmother told me about her wonderful obedient grandson who would not think of doing anything his parents would not approve of. One day his mother came into his room when he was eleven years old saying, "It is time for me to start restricting your television watching. I know there is something that can block out such programs, but can you show me how to work it?" Of course he knew how to turn it right back on. Did he or didn't he?

Here is another:

A son had his five-year-old daughter cleaning up poop from the backyard. The girl cried to her grandmother that she did not like that job. She said, "I am picking up dog poop all over." The grandmother responded, "WHAT?" She said to her son, "There are jobs and there are jobs, pick one for your child you would not mind doing yourself."

For most, grandparenting is a complete joy, feeling part of something very special while playing an important role in their lives. We can see life through their eyes. How golden is that?

SOME RECOMMENDATIONS FOR YOU:

- Respect their parents always.
- Keep disciplining at a minimum. You are their gift.
- Many children will act differently when they are not with their parents. You will want to tell the parents this. Better not to.
- Practically anything you dream up that is fun, kids will appreciate. One thing I learned: little kids don't like to walk far.
- If your grandkids are tattle tales and go back and tell their parents what you said, good or bad, be careful of your words.

QUESTIONS FOR PERSONAL REFLECTION

1. How have your grandchildren influenced your life?
2. Have you given up your own good time for the sake of being a good grandparent?
3. Would you not have had it any other way?
4. If you are a long distance grandparent, do you make an effort to see them or wait for them to come to you?
5. After a day with your grandkids, of course depending on their ages, how do you feel? One couple said to me; When they leave, "We go right to bed!"

It has been said that grandchildren are given to us so that we can correct the mistakes we make with our own children.

Notes

Part 5

Now Down to Basics

38

What Are You Eating?

Oops Have You Lost Your Waistline?

S ome of you might be saying, "What waistline? I haven't seen it in years."

Oh well, wherever it went, it will come back with one trick. You have to be mentally ready to change your eating habits for a lifetime. If not mentally ready, it can't be done. When the chocolate bar calls, or the pasta beckons, you have to be mentally ready to say no to it. Mental attitude is the key because your life, health and body are the most important thing in your life. Last night at a party, I was not in the least tempted to eat the potato pancakes, fried mozzarella and meatballs passed around on platters. I wondered why the guests were gobbling down and stuffing themselves with fat and salt? I am sure they were delicious to the taste, but I also knew how bad they would make me feel. "No thank you, forever."

On the street, one day, I overheard two friends talking.

"Can't wait to eat the fried chicken and waffles."

"Wow, sounds great," said the other.

Reminded of a diner scene at least thirty years ago, three (obese) people sat down next to me ordering the breakfast special, fried eggs, a high stack of pancakes, bacon and four slices of toast. The portions were large and they continued to smother the pancakes in gobs of butter and maple syrup. The jaw dropper came when they ordered apple pie a la mode for dessert. While this is an extreme example, those are the kinds of foods and combinations that must be forever eliminated.

Do you remember the days when you wore a tight belt around your waist, or slipped into a formfitting dress without covering it up with a jacket? The good news is, it only takes a few dedicated and disciplined months to get into shape. Isn't it great to know that you can achieve your weight loss in a relatively short amount of time? Isn't it great to know that eating poorly is a changeable habit and that your waistline is waiting to revisit you? I have a friend whose wake up call came when she fell off of a step stool into her closet. She fell softly, but she could not lift herself up; she was 40 pounds overweight. She felt helpless. She rolled onto her back, on to her side, her stomach, struggling to lift herself up. It took effort and time and when she finally did, she stood up frazzled, but with a new attitude.

"I vow to lose my weight, I refuse to put myself in a position of being helpless again because of my weight." To date, she has kept her promise and is losing pounds.

Here are some questions to ponder:
- Have you tried to diet only to gain back the weight you lost? Are you willing to give up some of your favorite foods that might be unhealthy?

- How badly do you want to stay in good health and in good shape?
- Do you prefer to socialize several times a week while drinking and eating in restaurants leading to late dining and going to bed on a full stomach? The early birds in Florida got it right. Eating a large meal after 7:00 P. M. might be fun and romantic but it causes weight gain.

The alternative to poor eating habits is to most likely be overweight, wearing pasta on your hips instead of that sexy outfit. If you do not want to give up the foods you love and have accepted being overweight, have you at least thought about the complications of being overweight? When we don't maintain a healthy weight, we become more vulnerable to disease. Diabetes is in epidemic form. Growing up, we didn't think we'd ever get old and out of shape. We didn't think that we might get ill, but the fact is we will if we do not take care of our bodies and in many cases it comes on suddenly. People don't become overweight overnight. The pounds creep up slowly, often unnoticed, until one day you look at yourself and wonder where that waistline went, and you run for the jacket to cover it all up.

If you are seeking to lose weight, flashback to the beginning and how your poor eating habits developed. Our moms were in charge of feeding us and most hadn't a clue about nutrition. When we had our children most of us moms continued the tradition of being clueless about nutrition. I fed my baby daughter so much that at one year old, she weighed thirty pounds. I thought it was adorable to pinch her doubled-over thighs, while expanding her appetite and taste buds far beyond what we now know is healthy eating. We went to elementary school where we learned reading, writing and arithmetic, but did we learn nutrition? Not at all. How could teachers teach us what they did not know? At school lunch, we were fed over-processed foods that turned to sugar in our bodies, followed by milk and graham crackers. Then there were the after-school brownies, French fries, and Coke that I looked forward to each day, learning to love sweets and not in moderation.

My parents owned a dress shop specializing in prom gowns. At age fifteen I tipped the scales at 150 pounds. Having beautiful dresses at my disposal and trying to zip one up was an ordeal. I was bulging out of the beautiful ballerina tulle gowns trying to find one that would fit, jealous of the pretty high school girls who were peppy and thin. They all seemed to easily slip into gown after gown at the Vogue Dress Shop, in Bayonne, N. J. during the early 1950s. There were mirrors from floor to ceiling in the store and our genius seamstress, Mrs. Golis, sat in the back turning a size twelve gown into a size six for the thin girls. (my parents did not like to lose a sale) My gown had to be let out to fit.

My parents finally sent me to a diet doctor, who put me on diet pills. I cannot remember if the pills worked, but do remember feeling dreadful and highly nervous on drugs. Back then, you either ate a lot and were chubby or you didn't eat that much and were skinny. My ex- husband, who was also a fat kid, had been brought up on roast stuffed chickens, chopped liver, knishes, eggplant parmigiana and spaghetti. My mother-in-law was praised as a gourmet chef. Oddly enough, my family were thought of as terrible cooks but without knowing it, they were the healthier cooks. They broiled the meat, boiled the potatoes, and opened cans of greens. Even so, the pounds piled up. My little sister Judy sat at our kitchen table eating everything that was served and remaining skinny. I dreamed of eating whatever I liked, a wish I still have to this day. My teenage years would have been more joyous had good nutrition been part of my life.

The first time I started to pay attention to my body was during pregnancy. Longing for a healthy baby, every precaution was taken to eat properly and take long walks each day. When it was time to give birth my body felt healthier and stronger than ever before and after birth my body was thinner than ever before. While I still knew little about nutrition, but vowing to stay thin, I lived on tiny portions of unhealthy foods; including a large amounts of chocolate for the day or just cheesecake which at that time kept me thin.

My kids were raised in a home filled with sweets, canned goods, processed foods and meat.

One day my 13-year old son came home and told me,

"Mom, I am now a vegetarian; I will no longer eat meat and some of the other bad things that you cook."

I was horrified. I prided myself on being a good cook and pleasing my family. Our dinner table fights were terrible. Finally, I said, "I will buy you the foods you want, but you will have to cook them yourself. I will not cook two different meals." We made a shopping list.

"What is that white thing in the refrigerator sitting in water?" I asked.

"Tofu, bean curd, Mom."

"Ugh."

I thought no more ham sandwiches in your lunch box? No bologna? Will he eat tuna fish?

Even with my son's influence it took years and years for me to learn a different way of eating. Finally after having a breakthrough it was becoming clear to see the difference between good food and bad food. It became difficult for me to put anything into my mouth that contained chemicals or was not wholesome. I began to eat fresh, natural and organic foods and have never gone back.

On her show, Oprah once put 60 pounds of fat into a bag and tried to lift it up. She could hardly do it. Every extra pound that I carry around, in my opinion, makes me look one year older. It is a chore to be heavy: clothes don't fit, walking is tiring, sitting is tiring and there is nothing glamorous or sexy about it. Well, you might say, who needs glamour or sexiness? You do! You were born to be sexy and to have sex. You were born to look the best you can at every stage of your life, living at a healthy weight and radiating beauty.

Jenny Craig, Weight Watchers, Zone, South Beach, and Atkins are waiting for you to call. There are hundreds of diets out there, all promising success and sometimes you can achieve long term weight loss. If you do achieve weight loss and are able to **keep** it off, it is most likely because you now started to think differently about food; you have finally changed your attitude. For others, diets are merely temporary measures. You might shed a few pounds at first, but once off the diet, steadily you will slip right back to your original weight. Following somebody else's thinking, but neglecting to change your own, is a sure path to failure.

Today, we are bombarded with every kind of diet and pill imaginable. Scientists and food gurus are constantly changing their opinions about what and what not to eat. How many times have you learned that something is healthy, only to have it be deemed "bad for you" the next year. Scientists are always learning or realizing a new discovery to help the population. Rather than feeling, there they go again, try to keep up with the times and changes. *According to the website Web MD, "'Diets don't work' is only half the story." Fernstrom states, "Lifestyle change will work if you have realistic expectations, good support, and choose a plan that you can stick with; a plan that will give you moderate change over a long time. That doesn't mean weight loss is easy. There's a myth, Fernstrom says, that normal-weight people can eat anything they want and don't need a strict exercise regimen but that's true for only a very small number of people. Most people who have a healthy weight have to work at it. "It is really hard to lose weight, and it is even harder to keep it off," Fernstrom says. "You can't cry about this. You must maintain hope. We just have to develop better strategies to keep people on track. The basic problem is that people think diets are something you do for a little while before going back to your old lifestyle." 1/10/11*

Calorie counting may be a smart weight maintenance strategy for some; however, it did not work for me because I enjoy huge portions. I felt sad "using up" 600 calories just for breakfast; how was I going to get through the rest of the day on a 1250 per day calorie count? It was depressing to know how limited my food intake would be. Some find it easy to have a small portion, take one bite of chocolate or one spoonful of ice cream. Me? I can eat six brownies at a sitting, an entire box of chocolates, and at least a pint of ice cream. I force myself to finish it all in one night so I don't have to face it for another day. Sugar craves more sugar. Putting weight on for me is easy, so nutrition and weight awareness is key. *In a new study reported in the NY Times (7/19/2011), Jane E. Brody states, "Counting calories may be outdated. Why? It depends on what calories you are counting. There are good foods and bad foods and the advice should be to eat bad food less. Eating in moderation might not work either. The study shows that just counting calories won't matter much unless if you look at the kinds of calories you are eating."*

I don't believe anyone likes to go on a diet. The good news is, you will never have to diet again if you choose healthy eating; you will only have to cut down on the amounts of food eaten if you do put on a couple of pounds. While I enjoy dining out, the ingredients of restaurant dishes are hidden and the bread baskets still too tempting. At home, it is easier to eat in moderation where the tempting fresh warm baked bread is not served.

When dining out, please don't be shy to ask about the ingredients in the food you wish to order; find out about the sugar contents in the sauces and gravies; how fresh is the fish; when and how did the fish come from the water to your plate? Has it been in the freezer?

NOW TO THE POINT:

Let me share how I found my way of a lifetime of healthy eating that works for me and perhaps for you too:

- Through the years reading labels became as natural to me as not reading labels.
- When the ingredients were not familiar it meant that the product was over processed and filled with artificial ingredients.
- Reading magazines, tuning into cooking shows where the emphasis was on healthy ingredients, rather than fancy fat producing gourmet dishes loaded with calories, became far more interesting.
- Vegetarian cooking courses and healthy foods cookbooks were exciting, and listening to friends who were far more knowledgeable than I was my best education.
- Noticing the foods people ordered in restaurants made it clear to me why they were out of shape and overweight.
- Learning about the chemicals in food and realizing the difference between healthy good food compared to what I had been feeding myself and my family clicked in. I started to shop in health food stores cutting out meat going to vegetarian to vegan and then swinging back to eating poultry and fish.

From Suzanne Sommers, an avid researcher, I learned a simple trick: to separate my foods. "Eat Great Lose Weight" will detail this way of eating. She was not the first person to endorse food separation, but she was the one that clarified to me how it worked. Suzanne figured out a way to get a waistline, and stay in good shape. Let me make it simple. Do you know what a carbohydrate is? Do you know what protein is? Don't eat them together. Example: Scrambled eggs (protein) cannot be eaten with toast (carbohydrate). Meat, fish and fowl (protein) cannot be eaten with carbs such as potatoes or rice. That is the trick. When you sit down to eat at home or in a restaurant decide if you are going to eat a protein meal or a carbohydrate meal. That goes for breakfast, lunch and dinner. I have been eating this way since 1998 and it works for me; not having to limit the size of my portions or counting calories is great. When I do gain weight it is easy to nip it in the bud by cutting the size of my portions while sticking to the same foods and back comes my waistline. A knowledge of good pure food and separating them is what has worked for me. If separating is not for you, then try a few bites of carbs when eating a protein meal and visa versa.

SOME RECOMMENDATIONS FOR YOU

- Nothing white, ever. That means no white bread, no white rice, no white pasta. Why? Because these foods turn to sugar in your body. There is one exception: a plain baked white potato without butter or sour cream. Remember: sugar will cause you to gain weight and put rolls around your waistline, quickly, I might add. "60 minutes" did a segment on sugar. Scientists are now learning that sugar not only makes you fat but it is dangerous for your health as it feeds cancer cells. I predict that they will now go after the sugar cane industry as they went after the tobacco industry. While one may think that if they cut out cake, cookies and ice cream they will have given up sugar. This is not true as the biggest problem with sugar is that it is contained in the many foods that you are used to eating such as breads, ketchup, mayonnaise, cereals; the list goes on and on. People for the most part do not bother to read the labels. You must learn to read labels.

- Learn to use spices. Forget the salt—shake the pepper more vigorously. Experiment with herbs and spices to enhance the flavor of your food. Bland foods can become exotic with the right seasoning.

- Forget candy, cookies, cake and yes, popcorn. No popcorn? How can I go to the movies without it? Believe me, it is not easy but instead bring in a salad, sliced turkey or chicken is great. Anything that will get you through the film without creating food smells. Will they let me in after reading this? Maybe twice a year a bag of popcorn becomes a huge treat. This might be an inappropriate place to write this or it might not have to do with healthy advice, but let me give you this tip: When they give you your bag, push the popcorn way down with your hand and then tell them to fill it up. At those prices you want a full bag, especially twice a year. The kids waiting on us don't care and are happy to fill it up for you. There is some popcorn that is healthy but I have not found healthy popcorn in most of the movie theaters.

- Greek yogurt 0% has really caught on and can be part of a healthy, balanced diet. Not all yogurts are healthy. It is important when it comes to yogurt to buy *organic non fat yogurt.*

  To ensure you make the healthiest yogurt choice, quick-scan the front label and then focus on the ingredients list. Stick with low-fat or nonfat varieties— you save fat and calories without sacrificing taste. Make sure the words "Live and Active Cultures" are printed on the container.

- Avoid front labels that say *light*– this is code for calorie-free artificial sweeteners like Sucralose, aspartame, and acesulfame potassium.
- Avoid highly processed sweeteners like high fructose corn syrup and sugar free and that goes for all foods.
- Fruit mixed into yogurt might taste good, but soon enough this will cause you to gain weight. Instead have plain yogurt (not vanilla) bought in a health food store, add your own fruit jam, or sweeten it with Stevia, a wonderful natural sweetener sold in health food stores. Throw away your chemical sweeteners. That is all that they are—chemicals.
- Enjoy organic corn flakes with organic yogurt rather than milk as our adult bodies do not need the milk of animals for our bones. Avoid milk and for that matter all dairy products for five days and see how you feel.
- Maya Angelou, the great poet and author, said, "If one craves a piece of pizza, a salad will not satisfy them; they will be dreaming of the pizza till they have it." If you find yourself in that situation, go ahead and satisfy yourself as long as it only happens now and then. For me, it is hot fudge. I just go ahead and have it. I order a small cup without the ice cream and feel happy and satisfied.
- Plan your home meals so you will not be tempted to grab food because you are hungry. Some people love to dedicate one day a week to cooking meals and freezing them so they have ready made dinners. This is convenient, especially if you work long hours.
- Don't stock tempting foods. No candy, nuts, ice cream, chips, white products ever in my home. If you live far from a grocery store, don't laugh, let someone hide those treat foods somewhere outdoors under a rock, out of reach and there for the day that you become desperate.

- Fruit can be fattening and cause bloating if you eat it after a meal. Many people think eating fruit after dinner is the better choice for dessert, only to find they become bloated with cramps. Fruit is tricky. Therefore, eat fruit alone and not as a dessert or in the form of a fruit salad. Mixing fruits can upset your system as well. Eat berries with berries, cantaloupe alone, citrus alone and avoid bananas as they contain sugar. Dried fruits are fattening so please avoid them as well.

- Two small squares of dark chocolate 72% cocoa is recommended a day. A high quality pure chocolate can lower the risk of heart attack and stroke by 39%. Chocolate should be eaten in moderation as it contains fat, but if you can limit it to the two squares, of course indulge. Another report came out where a square of chocolate is as good as cough syrup as it contains codeine but this I have not tried.

- Eat organic as much as possible. Cut down on red meat and dairy products or make sure these are organic. Non organic foods are infused with pesticides. While they are expensive, perhaps you can cut out other expenses, and put your money into healthy eating.

- Listen to your body. Are you really hungry or simply bored? Try not to snack. Have several small meals of healthy foods, but no packets of chips or a slice of pizza. Rice cakes are filling and the least fattening.

- Don't eat sandwiches. Have the ingredients that you desire without the bread, perhaps, making a lettuce sandwich. (a large piece of lettuce wrapped around turkey or such with mustard) Or try a rice cake instead. Buy your mayonnaise at a health food store made with safflower. Avoid the popular brands loaded with sugar. Use cold-pressed, pure olive oil. I use it for frying eggs, in salads and as a butter substitute for practically everything. Remember, we need oil to run our bodies. TIP: Buy a huge bunch of fresh basil, chop it up with a full head of garlic, add loads of olive oil and put in the blender. It makes a great salad dressing, seasoning for poultry and fish, and lasts a long time in your refrigerator. Coconut oil found in health food stores is good for us and enhances some dishes. Try a teaspoon of coconut oil in your oatmeal; it turns bland oatmeal into something yummy.

EATING FRUIT

This is informative! It has been circling the internet for many years.

"We all think eating fruit means just buying fruit, cutting it up and popping it into our mouths. It's not that easy. It's important to know how and when to eat fruit. What's the correct way to eat fruit? It means not eating fruit after a meal!

"Fruit should be eaten on an empty stomach. Eating fruit like that plays a major role in detoxifying your system, supplying you with a great deal of energy for weight loss and other life activities. Fruit is the most important food. Let's say you eat two slices of bread, then a slice of fruit. The slice of fruit is ready to go straight through the stomach into the intestines, but it's prevented from doing so, the whole meal rots and ferments, and turns to acid. The minute the fruit comes into contact with the food in the stomach, and digestive juices, the entire mass of food begins to spoil. Eat your fruit on an empty stomach, or before your meal! You've heard people complain: Every time I eat watermelon I burp, when I eat a banana I feel like running to the toilet, etc. This will not happen if you eat the fruit on an empty stomach. Fruit mixes with the putrefying other food and produces gas. Hence, you bloat! There's no such thing

as some fruits, like orange and lemon are acidic, because all fruit becomes alkaline in our body, according to Dr. Herbert Shelton who did research on this matter. If you have mastered the correct way of eating fruit, you have the Secret of Beauty, Longevity, Health, Energy, Happiness and normal weight. When you need to drink fruit juice drink only fresh fruit juice, not the concentrated juice from the cans or containers. Don't drink juice that has been heated. Don't eat cooked fruit; you don't get the nutrients at all. You get only the taste. Cooking destroys all the vitamins. Eating a whole fruit is better than drinking the juice. If you should drink the juice, drink it mouthful by mouthful slowly, because you must let it mix with your saliva before swallowing it.

"KIWI: Tiny but mighty, and a good source of potassium, magnesium, vitamin E and fiber. Its vitamin C content is twice that of an orange!

"APPLE: An apple a day keeps the doctor away? Although an apple has a low vitamin C content, it has antioxidants and flavonoids which enhances the activity of vitamin C, thereby helping to lower the risk of colon cancer, heart attack and stroke.

"STRAWBERRY: Protective Fruit. Strawberries have the highest total antioxidant power among major fruits and protect the body from cancer-causing, blood vessel-clogging free radicals.

"ORANGES: Eating 2 - 4 a day may help keep colds away, lower cholesterol, prevent and dissolve kidney stones, and reduce the risk of colon cancer.

"WATERMELON: Coolest thirst quencher. Composed of 92% water, it is also packed with a giant dose of glutathione, which helps boost our immune system. Also a key source of lycopene, the cancer-fighting oxidant. Also found in watermelon: Vitamin C and Potassium.

"GUAVA & PAPAYA: Top awards for vitamin C. They are the clear winners for their high vitamin C content. Guava is also rich in fiber, which helps prevent constipation. Papaya is rich in carotene, good for your eyes."

Find grocers who sell fine foods and who are keeping up with the times by buying organic or straight from the farm. Whole Foods, a nationwide chain, is remarkable and remarkably expensive. Their stores are jammed packed with people who eat wholesome food almost as if they can not get enough of it. Personally, I have never seen anything like the mobs of people scrunched in corners at lunch time devouring their Whole Foods lunch and dinner. I love the food chain, Trader Joes. They know what people need. They know what people like. Rather than ten different brands of a certain food, they choose one brand, possibly two to put on their shelves, simplifying your shopping and saving money. Once introduced to pure foods, people cannot get enough. Large food chain stores as well, are now becoming more health-conscious and offer many organic products. If you live in an area that does not have stores that fulfill your healthy needs, you might suggest products to your local grocer/farm or grow your own. When you buy local you can be sure that the food you're putting into your body is healthy, fresh, and good. The best produce you could ever eat or buy is local produce. In supermarkets there is so much to choose from, so many brands, and so many different types of food. How do you know if the food is healthy and good for you? When you stick to local produce, you can be assured that you are eating correctly.

Please note that shopping at health food stores does not mean you can overeat. I used to think that as long as I ate healthy food, it was OK to eat as much as I wanted until I blew up. You can get really fat on healthy foods as well, so the key is good nutrition, always in moderation.

SUGGESTED STAPLES:

- Organic eggs and egg whites. I buy organic egg whites separately; some people believe in having the egg whole all the time but for me, I enjoy eating egg whites in abundance and perhaps twice a week eating the whole egg. On his television show Dr. Oz stated eat eggs once a day. Your own doctor might not agree with him as mine did not.
- Hummus
- Plain organic yogurt
- Organic chicken
- Fresh fish (loving fresh flounder these days)
- Good whole grain bread (not whole wheat) and Pita
- Soy sauce, mustard, safflower mayonnaise
- Walnuts, natural almonds, sunflower seeds
- Greens, lettuce, tomatoes, kale, onion, garlic, peppers, cucumber, radish, greens, scallions, parsley, basil, cauliflower, broccoli, and any other fresh vegetables that are in season.
- Limited canned goods. Try tuna in water from a health food store instead of popular brands, also fancy tuna sold in jars. I also use organic black beans from the can when making my favorite recipe of Cuban black beans.
- Oranges, apples and grapefruit. In the summer strawberries, papaya, melon (cantaloupe, honeydew) and blueberries, blackberries, mango, peaches, apricots. Grapes and those awesome sweet cherries can put on the pounds.
- Oatmeal, organic corn flakes, brown rice, couscous, quinoa, whole wheat pasta, brown breads and pita are always on my shelf.
- A large bottle of cold pressed olive oil. Coconut oil is wonderful. If you do use butter, have the real thing. Stay away from substitutes.

- One healthy habit is to make a turkey and keep it in refrigerator as a slim snack. Go ahead, I dare you eat a whole turkey in one day.

NOTE: As with any new eating program, if you have a health condition, it is best to check with your physician before starting.

Food is medicine, food is energy, food is health. Once you begin to recognize the difference in foods and are able to understand your eating habits, you can now change and make a lifelong commitment to eating properly. The good news is that you can start at this very moment. Nature does not care about our hopes and dreams; it makes no difference to nature if we have good or bad cells or a colon or kidney that does not function properly. Nature does not care if we ate the brownie with ice cream last night. It will go on doing exactly what it wants to do right down to our inevitable death. We must outsmart nature every day of our lives by living healthy.

SOME ADDITIONAL TIPS:
- Eat when you are hungry, your body knows when. Please do not wait until you are ravenous when you will eat more and everything in sight.
- Best to eat little and often. You can eat five small meals a day, but no snacking.
- Cook at home as much as you can; you know what you are getting, fill that dishwasher often!

QUESTIONS FOR PERSONAL REFLECTION

1. Name the diets you have been on that simply did not work even though you followed them to a T. How long did it take to gain back weight? Would you go on that diet again?

2. Name one thing you could leave out of your daily diet. For instance, can you try substituting white bread with a sugarless whole grain (not wheat) bread? Can you substitute a fruit yogurt for a plain yogurt (not vanilla) Can you change from a saturated oil to olive oil?

3. Are you hiding underneath clothes and accepting it? How do you feel about your body? Do you use clothing to hide problem areas?

4. Weighing or measuring yourself every day is important. If you do not have a scale, try a tape measure. Will you commit to doing it daily even after reaching your proper weight?

5. The next time you go shopping for food, will you commit to reading labels and not buy it even if it has been one of your staples?

6. When did your poor eating habits begin leading you into losing your waistline? As a teenager? In the last several years?

Learning to eat differently is as difficult as learning a new language; this is no easy task!

Notes

39

Fasting/Cleansing

Give Your Belly a Rest

Have you ever tried fasting? Many people wonder: Isn't it dangerous not to eat every day? Wouldn't it be a shock to my system? Others might say, "I can understand that it could be fine for medicinal reasons but why else would I not want to eat?" Well, try it for a day or two and see why (*unless if you are under doctors care*). Fasting has helped me get started when I wanted to shed some pounds. Like any closet cleaning, it is a great feeling to take everything out, and then slowly put only what I want back into it.

Fasting is healthy thing to do for a day and if you can, up to five days. Your stomach needs a rest too.

In the Jewish religion, on Yom Kippur, we fast for religious reasons. Fasting is thought to have a significant spiritual benefit, helping us focus on our mortality and the value of life, while freeing us of physical concerns for one day so we can focus on our spiritual being There are many fasts within many religions. Some fasting diets involve drinking nothing but water or eating only raw foods for one or more days, while others restrict food on alternate days. Certain fasting diets only allow liquids like water, juice, or tea, while others dramatically cut calories but do not eliminate solid food altogether.

According to WebMD-Better information, better health: The leading source for trustworthy and timely health and medical news and information: Does fasting help you lose weight?

When you fast, your body is forced to dip into energy stores to get the fuel it needs to keep going, so you will lose weight. The big question is how long you will keep that weight off. Because food was often scarce for our ancestors, our bodies have been genetically programmed to combat the effects of fasting. When you eat less food, your metabolism slows down to conserve energy. Then, when you go back to your usual diet, your lowered metabolism may cause you to store more energy, meaning that you will probably gain back the weight you lost and possibly even put on more weight when eating the same calories you did before the fast. As you fast, your body will adjust by reducing your appetite, so you will initially feel less hungry. Once you have stopped fasting, your appetite hormones will kick back in. Some fasting diets claim that they can cleanse the body of impurities. However, there is no evidence that fasting detoxifies your body, or that your body ever needs to be detoxified. It is naturally designed to remove toxins through the skin (by sweating), liver colon. Copied from internet 1/15/2012.

If you decide to try it, by my experience get through the second day because almost guaranteed your head will become clearer and your body will feel light. The more days you fast, the better you will feel. I have gotten as far as day four and a half. The most difficult part of a fast is that most of us drink coffee or tea and the lack of caffeine even for several hours usually causes a rather unpleasant headache. This reminds us how addictive caffeine is and may be a motivation to switch to decaf. A perfect fast is lots and lots of water and nothing else. Grapes, melon watermelon make great fasts as well as cranberry juice that is unsweetened and pure.

SOME RECOMMENDATIONS FOR YOU:

- Start your fast.
- Get a healthy supply of your fasting foods into your home.
- If you are going on a watermelon fast, buy two large melons.
- If you drink coffee, Have a sip of caffeine in the morning and perhaps another sip in afternoon to avoid headaches. By the last of second day do not drink any caffeine.
- Rest along with your fast by going into nature and enjoying peaceful quiet days.
- You can go on a 3-day fruit-fast to cleanse your body. Eat fruit and drink fruit juice for just three days, and you will be surprised when your friends say how radiant you look! See chapter 2 for more on fasting.

QUESTIONS FOR PERSONAL REFLECTION

1. Have you ever been on a fast? What was your experience?
2. If you are trying it for the first time, how do/did you feel?
3. Are you willing to take in only water, to see what it might feel like at the end of that day, perhaps going into a second day?
4. Do you feel that not eating for one day or more is unhealthy?

"One quarter of what you eat keeps you alive. The other three-quarters keeps your doctor alive." This is a quote found on an ancient Egyptian tomb.

Notes

40

Vitamins:

They Taste Better Than Cod Liver Oil

We all struggle with which vitamins to take, when to take them and how many? It is important to buy vitamins made by a good company; the vitamins sold at drug stores don't have the same potency as those sold at stores that specialize in vitamins. Dr. Oz states, "If you've ever stood paralyzed in the vitamin aisle, facing the alphabet soup of supplements, fear no more. This is Dr. Oz's list of critical vitamins that every woman should be taking, and if you know your ABC's, this list should be easy to remember. *Hint: When buying your vitamins, check for bottles labeled 100% daily allowance on label.'*

Multivitamins fulfill your nutritional needs for the day. Take half in the morning and half at night. Multivitamins contain:
- Vitamin A – critical for healthy vision and skin.
- Vitamin B – a metabolism booster.

- Vitamin C – keeps your immune system strong, especially important during cold and flu season.
- Vitamin D – promotes healthy bones (and your immune system).
- Vitamin E – for healthy development of muscles and brain function.

SOME RECOMMENDATIONS FOR YOU

- Dr. Schulze's SuperFood 100 (essential) This fulfills my nutritional needs. I prefer this multi vitamin and it can be ordered on line; taken morning and night.
- Omega 3 1100mg fish oil (essential) this keeps your brain, heart and eyes healthy.
- Vitamin C 1000mg – keeps your immune system strong, especially important during cold and flu season.
- Calcium 1200 with Vitamin D (essential) This is important for women. I buy this combination at Vitamin Store. It does not hurt to take additional Vitamin D.
- B12 under tongue is also a good idea to take.
- I prefer taking my vitamins and other medications at bed time as well as filling in during the day and Dr. Schultz in morning.

QUESTIONS FOR PERSONAL REFLECTION

1. Do you take vitamins?
2. Have you noticed any difference in your health when you take them opposed to not?
3. Make a list of all of the vitamins that you take. The next time you see your doctor, go over the list to see what is truly necessary, can be added, or omitted.

Eating properly is the best way to attain proper nutrition. But the world of supplements are wonderful to make sure we are getting it right!

Notes

41

Drink:

Morning, Noon, and Night!

Water, water and more water. DRINK, DRINK, DRINK! Our bodies are made up of about 75% water that wants to pour in and out of us all day long. Drink to keep it replenished.

I always buy bottled water although it's debatable which brand is best. It is also debatable in some cities/towns if your tap water is just as good for you as bottled. For me, buying my water feels safer, besides from the enjoyment of drinking out of a bottle rather than a glass.

You might consider installing a water filter system, as schlepping bottles is strenuous and costly. They are easy to install and they can also hook up to your refrigerator icemakers. I also brought bags of ice home finding that unpurified ice had a refrigerator smell as well. Note: As of this writing I have installed a system in my apartment that is under the sink and hooks up to my refrigerator which makes my life easier and water less costly. There have been tests made by melting ice from a commercial freezer watching it turn brown. Commercial Ice machines are rarely cleaned. Of course it depends on where you live. NYC has good water as there is fluoride in the water which is supposedly good for your teeth.

We need to drink half of our body weight in ounces. So, if you weigh 130 pounds, drink 65 oz. of water per day or at least one liter. The more we drink, the better we feel. Water awakens our bodies; it is a rejuvenator that flushes our system. It's the ultimate cleanse. When you feel down and out like a wilted lily, drink water and watch yourself perk up.

However, as mentioned, it is not advisable to drink water while you are eating. It is best to drink a glass of water half an hour before a meal, and then waiting another half hour afterward. Except for wine, no beverage should be taken with food; it will distort the taste of what you are eating and you will bloat. Coconut water is extremely popular and healthy.

Coffee is fine as long as you keep it to two cups a day, and if you do not add sugar or packaged chemical sweeteners. There are many debates on how good/bad coffee is for you but everything in moderation is just fine. Try to avoid those exotic coffee drinks at Starbucks adding lots of calories. I love Starbucks but I am tea drinker.

Green tea is my favorite hot /iced beverage, but it does contain a small amount of caffeine, so please be careful if you wish to be caffeine-free. I love Starbucks' iced green tea and am hooked on jasmine green tea. One of the finest teas sold is Amanzi, as their flavors are pure and tea taste is distinctive from other brands. It is also the most potent so less is more, but I find it to be the most delicious. Amanzi is now opening up tea rooms in some cities. I also like Two Buds and a Leaf.

Try as many tea flavors as possible, sticking mainly to herbal teas to avoid too much caffeine. It has been stated that three cups of tea a day decreases heart disease and stroke.

White tea (recently introduced to me) is wonderful to sip and has less caffeine. I sometimes combine green and white tea in my morning tea

Hot ginger tea is good for colds and is suggested at the first sign of a sniffle or sore throat. If you are looking at tea as a health source do not add milk as it negates the benefit of tea. The amount of teas on the market is nearly infinite with tearooms and specialty shops springing up all over. Nothing is as delightful as afternoon tea out with a friend.

Fruit juices contain vast amounts of sugar. Buying a juicer and making your own is the best way if you like your fruit juiced. Healthy juice bars are good to frequent but only if they make drinks that are natural and pure.

Many of the smoothie places use canned or frozen fruit that contain, again, large amounts of sugar. If you are drinking pure carrot juice, leafy greens, beet or cranberry, then you are on the right track. If drinking fruit juice after a work out seems right for you, do check on the sugar and chemical contents. Orange juice creates acid and when combined in the stomach with milk, creates an imbalance in your digestive system as citric does not mix with milk lactose. Pour a half a glass of milk. Add some orange juice. Watch it curdle. It's not a good combination. There are many debates on this subject, both in favor and not, but for me it simply seems like a bad combination. I avoid orange juice altogether because of the sugar contents. I much prefer to eat an orange. Tiny oranges, cuties in season, that peel easily and are as sweet as candy, are a treat.

There are many good energy drinks out there but you must read the ingredient labels to find the best ones. Stay away from soda at any time. *According to Becky Miller Web Site: 6/15/2001 "The main ingredient in diet soda is water, specifically carbonated water. After that, the ingredients vary. For instance, caffeine is one of the more recognizable names on the list, but beyond that, the ingredients contained in diet soda sound more like chemicals than food—and, in fact, they are chemicals. Artificial flavors and colors, acidifying and buffering agents, viscosity-producing and foaming agents and preservatives all are present in diet soda."*

Yes, grant you occasionally, there is nothing like an ice-cold Coke but have it alone. Nothing tastes as good as the last Coke you had.

QUESTIONS FOR PERSONAL REFLECTION

1. Do you drink unpurified tap water? Would you consider filtering your water by installation or with a pitcher made to purify water?

2. Are you drinking more than two caffeinated drinks a day?

3. How do you feel when you miss a "caffeine boost"? Could you switch from coffee to tea?

4. Are you drinking grocery store fruit juice loaded with sugar?

5. Do you wait until you are thirsty to drink? The day may never come and you will find yourself dehydrated. Drink and drink more.

6. What was the best soda you ever had?

Notes

42

Smoking

Oh No, You Don't!

Smoking is a shameful thing to do to ourselves and others who breathe in our smoke. Once upon a time, and when up to three packs of Viceroys a day, I did stop. Quitting the addiction was not easy. It was the day of my father in law's funeral who died from cancer. Loving him as I did, my last cigarette went down the toilet after his funeral. **Everybody** can do it by flushing that last one away. The first three days you will wish you went with it, but that is all it takes; three little days to make your life endlessly longer without chemo for your dirty black lungs. Prior to that final day of smoking, I decided to play a game with myself as a test run. I would go back after two weeks proving to myself it can be done. Like anything else, such as food, we can stop if we really want to. It is about will power and changing our attitude on how we want to live our lives. One does not have to gain weight or go on to another vice using withdrawal of cigarettes as an excuse.

Nothing disturbs me more than having to breathe in cigarette smoke. Passing a cigarette smoker on the street and having to inhale the smoke is terrible. Smokers stand in front of buildings and we passersby have to inhale their habit. When driving, and the car in front of me has a hand hanging out with a cigarette at the end, with smoke blowing my way at a red light, is another terrible time of having to inhale. Then there are those who take their last puff at a bus stop and enter the bus, filling it with nicotine that is still on their breath and clothes.

One of the most frustrating times is when I carry the heavy props necessary for a day at the beach; find my spot, put the umbrella into the sand, sit back in my chair, and let out an "Ahhh!" Then there he or she is, lighting up a few feet away with the wind carrying their smoke right to me. Cruise ships now charge $250.00 if a guest lights up in their cabin. While I do not have road rage, I do admit to having cigarette rage.

The following is a story of how a cigarette smoker destroyed my home life. Our home is our refuge, our place to feel safe from the outside world. There is no place like home and when a cigarette smoker turned my home into hell, it was a living nightmare.

I lived in a breezy apartment in Miami and loved keeping the three large patio doors open, enjoying the fresh air. It was called a lanai apartment which meant it was on the pool level. Beautiful green hedges surrounded my apartment and the patio was filled with palms and lounge beds; almost like an outdoor room. My own private gate led to the pool and tennis courts. It was my own unique little cottage with all of the amenities of a full service building. At night I was able to sleep safely with my doors wide open enjoying the natural breeze. Thinking how lucky I was to live in such an environment where my creative writing and living could be nurtured came to a halt when:

"A smoker" moved in above me!

While smoke usually rises, a down draft brought his endless smoke onto my patio, into my apartment, settling into my lungs, changing my serene life. My dream home was going up in smoke. Introducing myself to him cordially and sympathetically I told him that I was receiving his smoke.

"I smoke," he said. "Close your door."

Not only was he a chain smoker, he was an arrogant man who smoked morning, noon and throughout the night. His sliding glass doors to his patio would slide open seven to nine times a day. He would step outside on to his patio, destroying my lungs, driving me insane. He smoked through the day and continued through the night. There was never a break. I would run to shut my doors, then open them, then shut them; the smoke waking me up coughing. I approached him again telling him I would pay the $550.00 cost of an air filter if he would smoke inside of his apartment. He said he would not think of harming his paintings or his computer by smoking inside, (better it be my lungs).

"Thank you for your offer. Close your doors."

I called my attorney to get some sound advice and he said, "Move."

"What move? How dare you say that to me! This is my home. We have to stop him."

I tried closing my doors, putting on the air conditioning that I disliked, but the stale smoke crept in. I bought three huge roaring fans that I placed on the patio hoping to divert the smoke. The noise was deafening. It helped somewhat but still no real relief. I thought of everything and anything that would help the situation. I took an extended trip to get away and clear my lungs. I thought about selling, but each time I thought of selling my gem, the breeze, the peace, my own garden, my heart broke. Appealing to the condominium board they considered it to be none of their business. I wrote a letter to the president and fellow residents begging for support. I considered going to the newspapers, even suing him for lack of quiet enjoyment every homeowner is entitled to have. I called the Florida legislature in Tallahassee's hotline to see if there were any ordinances against smokers in residential buildings. There were none. The only state close to addressing the situation was California. The president of our board, who was his friend, felt it was none of her business. The building was angry at me that I wrote a letter to the other residents. When I asked him again if he had any intention of not smoking out there, his answer was,

"Not anytime soon."

The unhealthy nightmare went on for eight months realizing there was no way out other than to move. But when, how, where? Coming home to the constant stench was terrible; hiding as I ran around my apartment trying to avoid his smoke made me crazed. Then, one day, my forty-four-year-old son, Roger, came to town. I said,

"I have tried everything. You are a son, he is a son. Maybe you can talk to him on that level."

Roger went right to it! "I know there is a problem," he said to the smoker.

"You have every right to smoke, but I am here to try to resolve your differences." He explained how the downwind brought the smoke to my apartment. The smoker began to understand the problem and started to blow the smoke in a different direction, the problem improved but still not completely; my home would never be the same. He truly did not care.

One day, there came a knock on the door. The smoker informed me he was starting construction in his apartment and wanted me to know there might be noise. The drilling and hammering went on for six months, and the smoking started again. There was no way out of this; the attorney was right, I had to move and I did.

I learned that the smoker also moved as there seemed to be an abundance of trouble for him in the building.

Cities now are changing their rules; smoking on NYC beaches might soon be outlawed, as well as in parks. I have one friend from childhood who smokes. If she was not my childhood friend I know I would not be her friend. However, when we do get together she is kind and considerate taking breaks to light up. I have tried endlessly to inspire her to give up cigarettes but she simply does not want to. Her mom smoked and lived until ninety-two and she plans to do the same. There is no one else in my circle of life that smokes. If I meet a person who does, why continue the friendship? I hope you too live a smoke-free life. As we all have learned secondhand smoke is just as dangerous.

QUESTIONS FOR PERSONAL REFLECTION:

1. If in the past you gave it up and are now smoking again, what factors contributed to picking up your visible weapon again?
2. Have you thought about taking one last puff and throwing it in the toilet and never looking back?
3. Have you considered a hypnotist? Hypnotists do work.
4. Are you afraid to give up cigarettes for fear of gaining weight or some other habit?
5. How proud are you from having given them up?
6. Do you stay away from cigarette smokers or are you tolerant of their habit?

Cigarettes: the visible weapon people carry!

Notes

43

Alcohol:

Is It a Sin?

I had a friend back in the 1960s who said, "Alcohol is sin." We would laugh and laugh at him as I guzzled down my gin and tonics. He might have been correct. What I think he was saying is that it is a sin to cover up your own personality by distorting it with alcohol and hangovers. In our teens, twenties and thirties we all want to experiment with drinks. I remember my friend, a perfectly wonderful mom, who we carried home drunk on a night out. To us, this was an exciting evening. If you hear kids talking today, their favorite topic is how much they drank the night before.

"I had seven beers last night." "Great."

"I had four gin and tonics; I was laid out. It was the best night ever."

Fifteen years ago I got drunk on Manischewitz wine at a seder and insulted my cousin Claire. I woke up the next day humiliated by my foul mouth and it was then that I said, "I will never touch alcohol again."

Cousin Claire gave me a gift of life. While I was never a problem drinker, I did not have the confidence to socialize with other people without having a drink, thinking I would not be nearly as much fun or able to enjoy my evening out. Our trips to the Bahamas/Caribbean years ago would always include a stop at the duty free shop, bringing home vodka, gin and other alcohol. Our home was well stocked for parties and friends. Now, I have bottles of champagne and liquor in my cabinet for years which I save for the guest who might enjoy a drink. Oddly enough that guest was me the other night. I decided for the heck of it to have a tequila straight up. Tequila is the purest of alcohol and causes the least after effect. I sipped it slowly, felt somewhat of a buzz and realized it was not doing anything for me.

Giving up alcohol has also changed my lifestyle. What is the sense of going to a bar or a cocktail lounge? Even parties can be dull. Non alcoholic beer tastes great or take me to a tea room instead!

While we can get away with a lot in our young years, drunk or tipsy at fifty, sixty or seventy it is not at all flattering and makes a person look older. A sober person can always spot an intoxicated person. Some slur their words and more often than not, get into a car driving themselves home, thinking an accident will never happen to them. It is sad to watch when you can do absolutely nothing about it until they change their own selves.

If there is something in your personality that alcohol brings out, such as anger or a loose tongue, you could end up feeling as low as I did with cousin Claire. Who needs the stuff?

On the other hand there is nothing wrong with having wine with dinner or a nice cold beer as long as it is pure enjoyment with little or no effect.

QUESTIONS FOR PERSONAL REFLECTION

1. Do you drink at home other than perhaps a glass of wine around dinner time or a beer?
2. Has consuming alcohol affected your life?
3. Do you feel you are not as good company as I did if you do not have a drink?
4. Have you tried to give it up, but much like what you eat, you cannot?
5. Do you ever drink and drive? What excuses do you give yourself for doing so? Would you get into a car with a driver who had several drinks?
6. Do you take responsibility for those you have entertained and have to drive home?

Keep your glass of wine with dinner to one, the best of two worlds. (Ok. Two)

Notes

44

Exercise:

Must You?

Yes you must!

Join the wonderful world of exercise, Just do it! Your body image and self-image are connected. In the 1950s we didn't know much about exercising except for our awkward gym classes. How funny we looked dressed in our little bright blue cotton suits with elastic around our thighs. We would march out of the locker room and form lines waiting for our teacher, Miss Zonic, to give us our orders: "Lift right leg, lift left leg!" We hung on to a swinging rope guessing that was a form of weightlifting then (and still a good one today). Nobody took it seriously and none of us liked gym. (Except for the cheerleaders and twirlers who were in top-notch shape, like my skinny sister Judy.) Aside from Ms. Zonic, the diet doctor who put me on pills would send me into his back room to exercise. There was a wooden seat that rolled over my rear meant to break up fat cells. It felt good to be in a sitting position, less work for me, having my rear tickled. There probably was a stationary bicycle, but not much else to remember. The room was lonely and empty, the equipment barbaric even for that time in a room never to be forgotten.

When Kennedy became President, we began to learn about exercise. My first work out was jogging, forcing myself to run around the park or up and down my street. It was difficult and hard on my body, especially the knees, praying the whole time for the run to be over. Jarring my body was not good, even though it did get me into terrific shape.

In the late 1960s, my husband took out a lifetime membership at Vic Tanny. I couldn't believe it, even though he was always ahead of his time.

On June 12, 1985, Victor A. Iannidinardo, an Italian immigrant's son who became Vic Tanny, the millionaire owner of the nation's first chain of gymnasiums and impeccably appointed health spas, died in a Tampa, Fla., hospital.

Although the gym went out of business it was well worth it as it put him in the right direction following a lifetime of exercise.

Now, we see a world of exercising people. Hundreds upon hundreds of gyms have sprung up all over the world. Personal trainers became a big business. There are home gyms and superb swimming pools in our own backyard. Wherever we go, there is a place to exercise and people working out. The question of the day became,

"Did you have a good workout?"

Cruise ships, for example, have added spectacular gyms for passengers to use and cruisers from all over the world use them as part of their vacation. In China, the parks are filled with hundreds of people doing tai chi early in the morning. The Chinese chose a healthy way of life for transportation as the streets are filled with bicycle riders rather than cars.

Most gyms make their money by signing up an abundance of members and banking on the fact that just a handful of them will use it regularly. Statistics have proven this to be true:

Health Club Statistics

Submitted By: Todd Sinett

Health Club Reality

Did you know the fitness industry structures their entire business banking on the fact that you will not exercise? Actual studies have found that the average gym user will go less than twice a week. What is that to say about us? Certainly, that exercise is not a priority. We are all busy; the planet has speeded up, and we are filled with projects with too many things to do each day. When it is time to exercise we are tired and lazy.

Airlines even tell us to first put on our own oxygen mask before helping others so that we are in a position of strength. Exercise should come first so that we are always in a position of strength. There are days that it does not seem possible to do any exercise; those days usually follow other days that you feel the same way. Exercise is a habit and when you are in the habit of doing it, it flows into your everyday routine and soon enough without some form of exercise the day is not complete.

Hopefully, you are not one of the gym members who do not go to the gym. Choose your exercise and consider it to be part of your life for the rest of your life: Swimming, walking, gym, climbing stairs, classes, skating, tennis, hiking, and lifting weights, with or without a trainer. What is it that will keep you interested and wanting to exercise at least three or four times a week? Pick your field and stick with it. It is good for you; it will clear your head, give you a high while giving you strength and longer life. We are supposed to eat three times a day, think how lucky we are that we don't have to exercise three times a day to keep us healthy.

How long should one exercise? That is your call, but it is suggested anywhere from thirty minutes to one hour, three to four days a week. Exercising more than five days a week is not necessary. Resting your body in between is just as important as working it, even though cancer research suggests 30 minutes of exercise a day.

Did you know that housework is one of the best forms of exercise? Bending down to clean and stretching to reach the high shelves to dust, dragging a vacuum from room to room, pushing your arm in and out to vacuum, squatting over a tub to clean it, and mopping floors are all beneficial moves for our bodies. Get out your broom if all else fails! Mrs. Bloomberg, mother to New York City's mayor, is quoted to have said, "If you drop something on the floor, when you pick it up, see what else is down there." After I heard this quote I noticed how much is down there.

Turn Housework into a Workout
By Dietitian, Juliette Kellow

According to a new survey by the Discovery Channel, many of us find cleaning our homes 'mentally therapeutic' and say it helps us feel in control of our lives. However, more than 40 percent of us believe we are addicted to cleaning and describe ourselves as 'cleanaholics'.

The average British woman spends more than 16 hours a week cleaning her home – that's the equivalent of 2 hours and 23 minutes a day!

Forget the gym! If women are really spending almost 2½ hours cleaning and tidying up every day, there's plenty of opportunity to get a sufficient workout without even leaving home!

Housework is a great way to burn calories. I remember being angry at my parents for lugging around a heavy vacuum and not having help. But as is the case with any workout, the more effort you put in, the greater the benefit. In particular, polishing, dusting, mopping and sweeping are great for keeping arms shapely. Bending and stretching, for example, when you make the bed, washing windows or doing the laundry are good for toning thighs and improving flexibility. And constantly running up and down the stairs as you tidy is a good aerobic workout.

Meanwhile, more energetic household chores such as decorating and spring cleaning, burn even more calories. Don't forget the garden either – weeding, digging, mowing the lawn, trimming hedges or bushes and sweeping up are all great muscle toners and calorie burners.

Check out our household activity calorie chart below, which compares the calories burnt by different household activities with walking…

Activity	Calories burned in 1 hour*
Walking at a moderate pace	287
Hoovering/vaccuuming	193.7
Dusting	173.6
Painting, Inside Projects	66
Gardening, Weeding	287.8
Mopping Floors	193.7
Car Washing	234
Cleaning Windows	180.3
Ironing	113.1
Wallpapering	133.2
Chopping Wood	415.5
Walking up & down stairs, moderate	516.3

* Values are based on a 37 yr old female, 5' 5", weighing 168 pounds. Those who weigh more than this will burn more calories; those who weigh less will burn fewer calories.

TOP TIPS TO GO FOR THE HOUSEWORK BURN

- Use a wax polish in a tin rather than a spray – you'll need to rub much harder to get a nice shine on your furniture.
- Don't leave things to pile up at the bottom of the stairs – take individual items upstairs as soon as you need to.
- Plan your housework so you constantly have to run up and down the stairs. For example, empty the dishwasher in the kitchen, then make the bed upstairs, then vacuum the living room downstairs, then clean the bathroom upstairs – and so on.
- Keep the laundry basket on the floor when you're ironing (rather than on a raised surface like a table). That way you'll constantly have to bend and stretch to reach the clothes. *Get more creative in the kitchen – peeling, chopping, stirring, whisking and beating all burn more calories than simply heating up a ready meal in a microwave oven. And if you really want to work up a sweat, have a go at making your own bread – kneading the dough is hard work!
- Stick on your favorite music and turn up the volume – it will help you polish and sweep that bit harder.

Here is a story of how I burdened myself one day. However, this is not recommended to anyone unless if you want to turn it into a completely insane good workout.

Picking up tiles for my contractor while re-doing my kitchen, I took NYC public transportation to the tile store in Brooklyn. With me was a plastic wheeled cart not quite anticipating the weight of the tiles. After picking up the order and walking across the street to the bus stop, I realized I could not lift the cart up the three steps of the bus. "Won't you please lower the handicapped platform so that I can wheel the cart onto the bus?" I asked the driver.

"That is for handicapped use only," the nasty bus driver said.

I stood with my foot on the bus. "My tiles and I are getting on to this bus, so I suggest you lower the platform."

He refused for the second time. "Not my problem."

At that moment while holding up the bus, I asked a passerby if he could please help me lift the cart on to the bus. He gladly said, "sure." He began to lift the cart up the steps as we both watched it completely break apart with the boxes of heavy tiles falling on to the top step of the bus surrounding the driver. It was overwhelming as the passerby fled. My cart was finished. Something like Sandra Bullock in *Speed*. I felt it would be impossible to ever get off of the bus. In my dilemma, I questioned the driver,

"Can I leave them on the bus and go home?" thinking I would get my car and drive to the bus depot at night.

"No way," the bus driver said.

I called the store where I had just purchased the tiles for help; they refused any assistance or rescue. Passengers sat and looked at me and the tiles sprawled on the floor, but nobody made a move to help.

After a few stops, I had to make my move. One angel woman picked up what was left of the boxes and tiles and helped me take them off of the bus a few at a time, along with the broken cart.

Now, everything was lying in the middle of the sidewalk in Brooklyn.

Someone suggested to get tape and tape the cart back together. All I needed was to get on the subway which would take me three blocks from home. The kind tape shop owner saw the cart and said,

"Tape will not hold it. I will help you."

He tied the basket with rope and placed the boxes back in the cart. It was heavy all right, but with two hands backwards,

I was able to pull it. Getting off of the subway, the wheels got caught between the train and the platform and another good soul yanked it off. The elevator brought me up to the street, now humbly grateful to be only those three blocks from home. As I started to walk, the cart began to fall apart again. The boxes were breaking, the tiles were falling out of the boxes, leaving a trail of tiles along the street. The wheels were now completely broken so I had to literally drag what had to be eighty pounds along the sidewalk in my broken cart with no wheels. As I pulled, more and more tiles fell out of the broken box. People were helping to pick them up as I lugged them along the yellow brick road. It was exhausting and excruciating. I am forever grateful to the doorman who said,

"Don't drag the tiles on the marble floor of the lobby." Surely it would have cost me thousands.

The point of telling you this story is that I made myself feel better by thinking of it as an exercise program. Whenever you are in a situation where you are doing strenuous work and resenting it, think of it as exercise.

"Why didn't you take a taxi home," a friend asked.

"It is not the nature of the beast; I thought I could make it!"

My exercise is water aerobics. Taking a class twenty years ago and continuing, with the underwater barbells and ankle weights is a great sport. Jogging in the water is much easier on the body. Water aerobics was always looked upon as "an old lady's sport," but not any longer. Young people are finding the benefits, as well as men. It is a terrific way to exercise if you like the water. One does not have to be a strong swimmer to participate; all you really need is access to a swimming pool, lake, or the ocean waves to make it even more fun.

Since water aerobics is a slower sport, it does not burn as many calories as you would compared to bike riding or any gym aerobics classes, however it is enjoyable and toning. Swimming a few laps, working the aquatic barbells under the water, kicking, twisting, walking, jumping as well as sit ups in the pool is a healthy work out. It is best to join a class and learn some routines and then if you wish, you can do them on your own. Perhaps you prefer lap swimming? All of the water aerobics equipment and instructions can be bought online made by *Keifer: www.keifer.com, 1-800 -323-4071.*

Walking is my other exercise. Most recently, I spotted a group of people with walking poles on the boardwalk of South Beach. I didn't realize that they were part of a class with an instructor, as I yelled out,

"What is that?"

They pointed to the instructor who seemed annoyed that I was interrupting his class. They were called Nordic walking poles. He explained that by walking with the poles, your upper body is getting as good of a workout as your legs. By the end of his class I ordered my poles and later turned out to be one of his best customers by buying them as gifts to friends. Europeans have been pole walking since the 1930s. It is something like cross-country skiing but without the skis, giving you a terrific upper body workout. Recently, there has been a revolution in the fitness world when it comes to pole walking. People will no longer venture out for their walk without their poles. They make you walk faster with more vitality, almost like you are flying. It is a cardio activity and still looked upon in the United States as a rarity.

One person yelled out to me on a beautiful spring day,

"We gotta get you some snow!"

The poles are versatile, lightweight, and portable, and airlines will check them in for free as long as you tell them that you need them for handicapped purposes.

Choose the activity you would like to do; get started with a friend if your motivation is on the low side, and consider what will suit you in the climate where you live. Taking a sixty-mile three-day walk for breast cancer in Miami proved to be inappropriate, as people could not do their best in the city's heat. Climate should enter into your choice of exercise.

Better still, if you can afford it hire a trainer and do weight lifting. It is a worthwhile life time investment. It is great for strength plus the wonderful dents it gives most in their upper arms. If you find that you are exercising, but irregularly, start a program and try to make it your priority with a new attitude. Much the same as with eating, you have to be mentally ready to commit.

QUESTIONS FOR PERSONAL REFLECTION

1. Are you willing to take a twenty minute walk to get started?
2. As a kid, was there something you enjoyed doing that you can bring back into your life? Skating, running, jumping, horseback riding etc.
3. Make a list of any types of exercise that might hold your interest and try each one out for ten to twenty minutes to see if it is something you will continue.
4. Are they seasonal such as skiing? What exercise you can enjoy on a daily/weekly basis?
5. Can you ask a friend to join you to motivate each other during an exercise?

The best thing to do when you get out of bed in the morning is to straighten up your home; it will straighten you right up!

Notes

45

Yoga and Pilates:

Strike That Pose!

The very act of meditation is a great joy. Just to be able to dance, just to be able to sing, just to be able to sit silently and breathe and be, is more than enough. —*Osho*

My yoga practice started about thirty five years ago. If you were in my class today, you would think it was my first day even though keeping up with the poses is not any problem for me. My body simply is not flexible but what would it be like if I didn't do yoga at all? Yoga teaches us peace and alignment above all. If you come in with an ache or pain, it is almost guaranteed you'll leave without it. Yoga is wonderful for tight bodies and wonderful if you are fortunate enough to be flexible. My parents would complain about their legs and feet and how much they hurt. We took it for granted that is what happens when one gets older; if only they'd known about yoga and stretching. Hot salt baths were the only means of stretching muscles for my parent's generation, and though a hot bath is always delicious, it's simply not enough.

There are many forms of yoga: hatha, kundalini, bikram, integral, vinyasa, etc. Hatha was the first yoga introduced to me and it seems to offer simpler poses than other styles.

These days, hatha is most often used to describe gentle, basic classes with no flow between poses. A hatha class will likely be a slow-paced stretching class with some simple breathing exercises and perhaps seated meditation. This is a good place to learn beginner poses, relaxation techniques, and become comfortable with yoga."

"Many people think that yoga is just stretching. But while stretching is certainly involved, yoga is really about creating balance in the body through developing both strength and flexibility and breathing. This is done through the performance of poses or postures, each of which has specific physical benefits. The poses can be done quickly in succession, creating heat in the body through body movements or more slowly to increase stamina and perfect alignment. The poses are a constant, but the approach to them varies depending on the tradition in which the teacher has trained. Yoga has become a fashionable lifestyle pursuit appealing as much to competitive marathon runners and college students as is does to om-chanting meditators. It is a 5.7 billion dollar business."

Chanting and reciting OM was once extremely amusing to me. My mom and I went to a class and remember lying on the floor next to her, giggling during the session. What were those strange new sounds, the OMs, the chanting recited hundreds of times? What were we doing in such a class? We were learning about something completely foreign to us.

While it is enlightening to find out about our inner essence, there are those of us who find it downright scary to step into another zone that is different or unfamiliar.

About twenty years ago a spiritual center was started in Miami Beach. They offered free classes on breathing, meditating, healing, and reiki. The freebies attracted many people. However, when they started to charge a fee, the attendance dropped drastically. People did not want to pay for spiritual growth; they would pay for movies, theater, shows, restaurants, parties, disco, but not spiritual growth. When Oprah came along introducing people who wrote brilliant books on following a spiritual path such as Eckhard Tolle and Deepak Chopra, people began to wake up. The yoga center in Miami Beach became crowded with teacher training classes. People went to India and brought back their knowledge; an enormous explosion took place in cities and that owner suddenly had an extremely profitable business.

Now yoga is a way of life, another way to exercise our bodies. Mats are carried all over town by students on their way to classes. Still, spiritual growth such as yoga and meditation is still limited to a great extent to the few who care to go deeper into their souls or have curiosity into other ways of life. Yoga practice leads us into many directions especially peace. When we are at peace as yoga practice teaches us, our minds become clear and we see things differently. We become more creative, softer, kinder while developing patience.

Start with a beginner's class if you have not yet tried yoga. You might not ever graduate from that level, as the beginner level is the most relaxing and that is fine. If you like more challenge you will want to go on to other levels. Beware of the yoga teacher who pushes you. Many teachers try to get you into positions that are not right for your body. **Remember, this is your body and don't let anyone tell you how it should**

work. I suffered two terrible accidents by not following that rule. The first teacher had me lie on my back with my knees pulled towards me. He wanted to give me a better stretch, so he pushed and pushed my knees deeper in towards me until my back cracked. I could not get up. It took months to heal. The second teacher told me to put my legs up against the wall and I came down with a thud, spraining my ankle. Allowing a teacher to do what she/he thinks your body should do is not a good idea. Think for your own self and don't let anyone push you if you feel resistance in your body. Tell the teacher,

"I am doing my best and I prefer not to be touched."

My yoga practice has led me to spiritual retreats /ashrams and there is nothing like going to one for the best "feel great" time you will ever have. At the beginning, the early morning wake ups, chanting, meditation and long robes were hard to accept. The accommodations were simple to say the least; usually sharing a room with another seeker, bathrooms were down the hall or outside. But each time, I came home more fulfilled, different, excited to be on a path towards a healthier lifestyle. At the retreat, they did not allow caffeine because it is a severe drug and only when we abstain can we understand the difference. I was a four to five cup a day drinker and withdrawing gave me an excruciating headache that lasted for two days. When it finally went away, I never wanted to go through that pain again and never did.

At the retreat they served healthy vegetarian food and I thought nothing of piling my plate sky high, learning quickly healthy food too could make me sick and gain pounds.

Once in the routine, living simply was the way to go! From early wake ups, to a walk in the woods at day break, to a yoga class, meditating, healthy food, no sugar, no caffeine, gardening or helping in the kitchen with lots of rest felt wonderful. In the evening there was chanting, prayers and early to bed.

I met new people with new ideas who lived their lives in this manner with vocations such as body healing, massage, facials, dance. Those who took the intense worldwide yoga teacher training courses to become a certified instructor found it to be one of the toughest courses ever. Swamis who dedicated their lives to peace and running the establishment were great interesting guys.

"Swami means master. It means striving for the mastery over ones smaller self and habits, so that the eternal self within can come shining through. A swami is a monk who has set aside all of the worldly pursuits, so as to devote full time and effort to the direct experience of the highest spiritual realization and service to others."

On holidays at ashrams there is always a special ceremony where guests can perform. My friend is a professional belly dancer who danced with beauty, grace, and style in a gorgeous costume that was somewhat revealing. Her movements were beautiful to watch and she would dance that evening. The music played and she began to dance in front of the Swamis. The poor Swamis hardly knew where to put their eyes trying to be respectful. We all agreed that perhaps it was not a good idea even though the audience adored the dancing. It was a story not to be forgotten.

At peace we can make clear decisions and solve life's problems. Healing a relationship or figuring out what has kept us from moving forward becomes clearer. Meditating is an amazing tool especially when it works; by that I mean when we can let go by going deep inside of ourselves, it is transforming. However, it is sometimes difficult to arrive in that state if you are unable to let go. It takes practice; personally I have used meditation in some of the strangest places. For example, waiting in a long line and growing agitated, or in a concert or movie that is boring with no escape. Sometimes when I am really pissed, I use mediation. (Mind you, you must learn a mantra; a word that is repeated

several times over again, that brings you into a meditative state.)
I received my mantra at thirty years old while sitting before a
guru swearing to secrecy that it would never be disclosed to
anybody and keeping that promise forever.

Also on a side note: watch out for your shoes. Shoes are
not allowed in the temple of worship and one evening I came
out and found my shoes were gone. Just because one practices
spirituality doesn't mean they are honest!

Add a retreat to your way to holiday and while going to
a 5-star hotel, with room service, lots of croissants, gourmet
food and comfortable lounge chairs in the sunshine at a pool
or beach are all wonderful, you will learn more about yourself
at an ashram. Depending on the city you live, you can Google
ashrams. There are some amazing places in the Bahamas,
Hawaii, Costa Rica as well as miles from your own home. My
favorite is Sivinanda Yoga Retreat.

Pilates is another wonderful practice. It is great for our abs
and alignment and does not require the major flexibility of
yoga.

*"Pilates is a form of exercise, developed by Joseph Pilates, which
emphasizes the balanced development of the body through core
strength, flexibility, and awareness in order to support efficient,
graceful movement."*

Pilates is one of the most popular exercise systems in the
country. Now it seems like everyone is either doing Pilates or
interested in starting a Pilates exercise program. Indeed, one of
the best things about the Pilates method is that it works so well
for a wide range of people. Athletes and dancers love it, so do
seniors, women rebounding from pregnancy, and people who
at various stages of physical rehabilitation.

The benefits of Pilates are numerous. It makes one feel
stronger, longer, leaner, and more able to do anything with

grace and ease. It somehow narrows your body. In the past several months I have become addicted to pilates. It is not easy, but invariably when the class is over I feel renewed, agreeing that I am straighter, stronger, more youthful and am able to go about my day feeling better. The practice did not come easy. However, I am proud to say that my teacher went away for a long while and when she returned, she remarked.

"I see you have been doing pilates, there is a great change in you."

CORE STRENGTH

Core strength is the foundation of Pilates exercise. The core muscles are the deep, internal muscles of the abdomen and back. When the core muscles are strong and doing their job, as they are trained to do in Pilates, they work in tandem with the more superficial muscles of the trunk to support the spine and movement.

*As you develop your core strength you develop stability throughout your entire torso. This is one of the ways Pilates helps people overcome back pain. As the trunk is properly stabilized, pressure on the back is relieved and the body is able to move freely and efficiently. (After class my back feels terrific, (unfortunately pilates does not **cure** a* bad back, but it does help the situation especially after a class.)

The Six Pilates Principles are centering, control, flow, breath, precision, and concentration. These principles are essential ingredients in a high quality Pilates workout. The Pilates method has always emphasized quality over quantity, and you will find that, unlike many systems of exercise, Pilates exercises do not include a lot of repetitions for each move. The instructor usually says, last six, five, four, three, two, rest. which sounds great when you are in a difficult pose. Doing each exercise fully, with precision, yields significant results in a shorter time than one would ever imagine. I find doing less repetitions is wonderful.

Core strength and torso stability, along with the six Pilates principles, set the Pilates method apart from many other types of exercise. Weight lifting, for example, can put lots of strain on arm or leg strength without attending much to the fact that those parts are connected to the rest of the body! Even running or swimming can seem like all arms and legs, with either a floppy or overly tense core. Ultimately those who really succeed at their sport learn to use their core muscles, but in Pilates this integrative approach is learned from the beginning.

Pilates exercises are done on either on a mat on the floor, or on exercise equipment developed by Joseph Pilates. The reformer is probably the best-known piece of resistance equipment that you will encounter at a Pilates study. It is done with an instructor either privately or with two or three others. It looks like a large wooden table and has equipment attached to it that will tone your body with pulleys and resistance from the participants own body weight. Pilates is best learned through a combination of classes and home workouts. You can get started right away. with tapes or purchasing a pilates machine.

QUESTIONS FOR PERSONAL REFLECTION.

1. If you have not tried yoga or pilates, is it something you might consider?
2. Are floor exercises difficult for you? Did you know that many teachers use chair exercises?
3. If you have been to an ashram, what benefits did you receive; did you make any changes to benefit your health?
4. Do you find being in a class where people are more flexible than you intimidating? How might you conquer this?

Yoga/pilates is not a contest; only to be done at your own pace for your own benefit and enjoyment.

Notes

46

Fashion

What's On Your Plate?

Are you a trendy dresser, sporty dresser, one who prefers a little black dress, a labels-only girl, or one whose style is eclectic—a little of this and a little of that? Maybe you have simply resorted to wearing your workout clothes where ever you go. Have you? When do you feel your best, what style mimics your personality? Bill Cunningham, a fashion historian, says:

"Fashion is the armor to survive the reality of everyday."

As we know, clothing is one of the necessities in life so we might as well enjoy the clothes we wear. Why be lazy by not looking great and stylish **every day** rather than dressing to simply keep us decent and comfortable. Some of us look to turn heads and be trendsetters, obsessed by what to wear, staying home rather than venturing out by not looking anything less than perfect, others are quite the opposite. Going into a large department store and seeing endless racks and bins of clothing amazes me. How will they ever sell all of those clothes? There are clothes to suit everybody, the choices are vast and it is up to us to learn and choose what flatters us the most. Learning how to do that is a study. Some have a good eye to spot their style, others need a good deal of help from salespeople.

How do you enjoy a shopping day; alone or with somebody else who can help make decisions? Shopping alone and letting my own mirror at home be the judge is my thing! Although, sometimes things look great in my own mirror, yet catching myself in an outside mirror has made me run back home to quickly change. I have made plenty of my own mistakes such as being overdressed or underdressed at a party; skirt too long, too short, bra straps sticking out, underwear line noticeable, losing underwear that falls down with too loose elastic. How many of us have made a faux pas by being too underdressed or overdressed at a party? We have all heard those "horror stories" of spending money on a dress and before our very eyes it has been copied down, sometimes even before we wear it or meeting someone at a gathering wearing the same dress and she looking better in it than you do!

Sometimes we do not realize our mistakes until years later when we look at ourselves in photos. I will never forget the mistake made out on one of my first dates after separating from my husband. He was handsome, eloquent and rich and I tried to dress to impress. He had met me looking trendy in jeans and a black tee shirt but I chose to wear fancy loose pants with sequined sides that were expensive but totally inappropriate for where we were going. On top I wore a sleeveless blouse but did not realize my bra straps were sticking out. My outfit was a disaster. I changed my image by overdressing and the date was a complete flop especially when he tucked my hanging bra strap back into my blouse, which humiliated me. Then there were times while looking great from the front, the back of my hair had that empty hole and my clothes a bad fit. Our backs are equally important to check. I once went to a funeral in a mini skirt because it was black, and looked absolutely ridiculous. Mistakes, mistakes, we all make them. Shopping is not easy; it can be downright exhausting. My daughter told me of how she went into Century 21, a great fashion store in NYC in the morning.

"Mom," she said, "when I came out, it was dark."

Wearing someone's label has never been my style (why walk around wearing clothes with someone else's name on it?) I greatly admire designer clothes and the few that I have bought have lasted the longest without ever going out of style. However, creating my own look is the most fun and clothes should be fun. Restyling and experimenting with something such as cutting off sleeves, shortening a dress into a top, lengthening and adding another pattern at the bottom works; and belts are wonderful for forming the body. One day in my apartment I was barefoot and messy wearing old bell bottoms and a top with my hair in rollers. Having no time to change, I kept adding to my old bells, high heels, then a shorter top as a layer, a white painted necklace, a stunning colorful bracelet, and a red shawl.

Perhaps you have arrived at an age and you are more than fifteen pounds overweight, your hair is shorter than you ever thought it was going to be as you no longer want to be bothered and you are wearing a large tee over comfortable baggy pants and flat shoes. You have given up on style and no longer much care about how you look. Where has that sexy lady gone?

Then again, perhaps you have arrived at an age and you are thin, nicely toned, you wear a flattering hairstyle hardly looking your age, yet your clothes are for an older person than yourself. Your belief is that a fifty plus woman should look conservative, not wear color or trendy styles. You consider yourself old and dress accordingly. In both of these situations you have lost your ageless spirit. Repeated through my book are the words, "Growing old does not mean being old or looking old."

When we are growing up, our taste begins to develop. We might be fortunate enough to have a mother, a mentor, or a classmate who we admired. My young seventeen year old grandson is now learning style, primping and checking mirrors in his new young man look and learning good taste. I loved watching one of my classmates come to school. She was petite, popular and pretty, prancing into class wearing colorful cashmere sweaters and long ballerina skirts. Her orange short sleeve cashmere sweater and long dark brown skirt is locked into my memory. It can take many years to learn what looks best on us, to learn what colors are the most flattering, what length is best, how to tie a scarf, or how to add a pin or earrings. We are all different, unique, and it is all about creating our own style.

There are people with no fashion sense whatsoever and suddenly they become fashion plates by educating themselves into the world of fashion. Who is to say that one cannot continue to wear youthful styles throughout life especially if we have taken care of ourselves. The ingenious chain, "Forever 21" says it all. We might have to put restrictions on details like hemlines and necklines, but looking dowdy is *not* what "Amazing Ageless You" wants to be. Forever 21 and H&M is now saturating the market with clothes that are stylish without being expensive. While they may be focused on youth, they are meant for all generations. We are fortunate to live at a time where we can buy online, so even if a store is not in your vicinity you can look it up on the internet placing an order that comes directly to your front door.

Do you notice that some people simply look good in everything while others struggle? How unfair life is! Some people make clothes come alive no matter what they put on.

There is little that we can do about our bone structure except to accept it and to be who we are. Many women go shopping and buy the season's latest even if they do not have the right bodies to carry off the new style. For example, a long skirt might be the now thing but if our bodies look better in a shorter skirt, what is the sense? So while it is great to buy what is in vogue, make sure it is a style that flatters your own body.

At any age, you can dress with spunk and color. Clothes are fun and should be fun. Looking disheveled and out of style is not part of living an ageless life. If you own an item that does not make you feel good, get rid of it; somebody else might enjoy it. That goes as well for brand new mistake purchases which we have all made. Experts say if there is something in your wardrobe that you have not worn in a year's time, give it away, especially when it comes to uncomfortable shoes that are killing your feet. Ouch! Some people make pacts with themselves, especially when it comes to tee shirts. For every new one they buy, they give one away.

Low cut necklines as long as the skin is not sun-damaged are wonderful. We have to be careful if we have those terrible brown sun spots or a wrinkled chest caused by sun damage. It is best to wear clothes with higher necklines and longer sleeves if that be the case. Brown spots and wrinkled chests are unappealing as well as moles. I have a friend who will not give up her freedom in clothes by covering up.

She said, "I refuse to cover up my freedom."

She wears sun dresses in summer and short sleeves in winter. Unfortunately, there is little to be done if you let your skin go too far. Would you approve of you if you saw your clone in the mirror? If your skin is lovely, buy that lift-up-squeeze-together bra and lift your breasts. Breasts are gorgeous and sexy; love them, enjoy them, and expose them in flattering necklines; sex is always in style and one is never too old to be sexy; show your legs and enjoy your lovely spotless or clothed skin at any age. Then when you go to the beach, enjoy your exposure and stay under an umbrella.

Women often find it quite amusing to evaluate and critique what a friend or celebrity wore. The age-old question among girlfriends is, "How did she look?" We watch awards shows to see who won but even more importantly to see the clothes celebrities wore. We telephone girl friends, praising or ridiculing "what she wore, how she looked," and hearing their views. We love to see the celebrities we admire and fashion disasters of the week. Fashion is a great pastime. Designers are always busy getting their newest lines intact. Some people wait with bated breath for designers to show us the look and colors for the next season. We read fashion magazines showing us new styles and ways to improve our selves; it is fun to pick up tricks that we can adapt and that work to enhance our own image. We follow models, and long to go to Paris or Milan to pick up just one new thing that might set us apart from others.

On the other hand, what is more fun than shopping in a thrift or consignment shop? Sometimes it is a boost to buy something for one or two dollars and say goodbye to it the next week. Wearing the most gorgeous black velvet gown to a few eloquent affairs bought in a thrift shop for fifty dollars was a smash. It was a black velvet tight fitting strapless fish tailed bottom gown that came with long black velvet and pearl-trimmed high gloves. When you shop in a thrift store, it is best not to wear everything together. Be subtle adding one piece of clothing or jewelry at a time, blending it with your other clothes. Too much of a good thing is never good. Other discount stores like Target or Kmart are also great for workout clothes. I also like American Apparel for workout clothes which is not a discount store.

Which colors look the best on you? When did you last receive a compliment wearing a certain color? There are simple ways to find out. With the Internet (the "new Ouija board," as I call it), we can Google anything and get answers. For instance, Google "color test" and you will get many sites to visit. Discover sites that you find beneficial and visit them often. "*E how*" seems to give a vast variety of ideas. People blog about everything. If you Google "fashion blogs" you will find hundreds to read. You can learn what colors are hot this season by watching television or looking at a fashion magazine. My favorite magazines are *Bazaar, Elle* and *In Shape*. We live in a world of Technicolor so don't be afraid to wear it. Basic black is forever gorgeous and eloquent but color brightens everybody's day, especially your own.

WikiHow, a great internet site states: "Don't just stick with colors that go with you; you can either go with the flow or you can go wild. Don't be boring, remember to be yourself, and since there is no one that is exactly like you, you will definitely stand out. Although you should stock up on colors that enhance your skin tone, don't be afraid to toe the line. It is also important that you wear colors that flatter your features. Choose different shades of non-complementary colors if you want to--your fashion is all about you--but use them in moderation. If orange is your favorite color but doesn't look good with your skin tone, for example, maybe wear an orange belt with a blue shirt, or any other color that both looks good with orange and looks good on you. If you are not a fan of bright colors, you can spice up even a neutral color scheme. If you are safely wearing black, cream, brown, and blue, add a colorful scarf or shoes of a different color."

My grandmother always wore pastels, yellow, pink, and blue dresses with matching shoes and lovely jewelry. She always looked bright and beautiful and, in her case, had a disposition to go with it. I never saw her in black except at her daughter's funeral--the tragedy of my youth. She did not remain in black for long, She married twice afterwards and went right back to her colorful clothes and bright smile. While she was devastated, I remember her sadly telling me, "There is nothing in life that you cannot get used to."

I most enjoy shopping when I travel. There is nothing like a shopping spree when you are relaxed with plenty of time. Some people travel with a half-empty suitcase so they can fill it up on their way home. In a taxi on one of my trips, I passed a shop with a red necklace that caught my eye and was determined to find that necklace. My afternoon was spent walking up and down every little winding street finding that gorgeous $10.00 necklace, as it turned out. Ordinarily one does not have that kind of time. To name a few destinations for buying clothes, Vietnam is on top of my list. Holan city is worth the visit where silk suits made to order are classic. Mine is about fifteen years old and it still looks great. My daughter went to Bali twenty years ago on a vacation and fell in love with their children's clothes. While all babies were wearing pink and blue, the clothes she found were batik in fabulous bright colors. Her business is still thriving, her website is called "Back from Bali. com." Plug! There you will see unusual colors and style for kids. Travel lends itself to more unusual things. India has fabulous styles. I now own two unusual jackets; brocade and peach silk. While France and Italy used to be the best places to shop, the cost to Americans now is almost prohibitive. Almost anywhere that you travel out of the country there is always something to buy that is different and more interesting than what you find at home. However, be careful of buying something ethnic that looks ridiculous in your own hometown. If you are not a lover of shopping, try shopping on an off beat morning where discounts are awarded, or when the store is getting ready to close and there are fewer shoppers.

If all else fails, try the Miami Walgreens and CVS stores. They have great beach ponchos and tops in vibrant colors that have enhanced my summer wardrobe.

There is nothing worse than feeling pressured and needing an outfit for a particular occasion. Therefore buying when you do not need something and putting it into your closet to appreciate when you do need it, can be a blessing and save you time and stress. That goes for gifts; buy them when you see them and stash them away for an occasion.

Learn how to dress with style by experimenting and having fun.

Here are some different ideas:

- Do not be like the woman at the party the other night, who said, "Why bother, nobody looks at me." She looked stylish and attractive but she had lost her spirit. People will look and admire her as I did, if her ageless spirit is turned back on.

- Turn a jacket inside out. Sometimes the linings look better than the outer material itself. *Some clothes look better backwards depending on your posture. Way before Celine Dion turned her white tuxedo jacket backwards at an award show and created a large stir, I was wearing many clothes backwards including my tuxedo style jacket. This year I turned my twenty-six-year-old falling apart mink coat inside out; now it is a fur-trimmed satin coat and looks great. If your lining is in good condition, give it a try. If something misses looking good on you, try turning it backwards and see if it works. Depending on your posture, some clothes look better that way; you be the judge. The same goes for lengths as my pants and dresses look better a bit longer in the back because of the way I stand. Sometimes a tee shirt looks better worn backwards.

- There is nothing as classic as Ralph Lauren: jeans, boots, white shirt, sweater or jacket; his styling cannot be matched.
- Remodel an old coat by adding large contrasting buttons or cut off the sleeves to make a cape effect.
- A tuxedo jacket and a silk shirt should be part of your wardrobe.
- Shop outside the box such as the Christmas tree base cover trimmed in gold that I bought as a gorgeous cape.
- Wear jeans with the most elegant jacket you have, as well as with high-heeled shoes. Try not to follow trends or try to fit in with everyone else. Remember, be the leader not the follower. Fads come and go quickly. If you must try out a fad do it with a hat, a belt, a scarf, add a shawl or new accessories that go with your look. The shamoose dress was a terrible fad; the oversized shoulder pads in the 80's are a trip to look at in photos feeling we looked big and powerful. Surely, if they come back in style we probably will wear them again. That's what stylish fads are.
- When you are in a place where there are hundreds of people, such as a city or airport look at people and how many different styles there are and how each person is so much of an individual.
- Wearing a tee and then putting a blouse over it is not flattering to most women because it does not hide what you are trying to hide; it simply creates bulk. Wear the blouse or wear the tee; this is a popular mistake.
- Wear a jacket with a short skirt and black tights or even better barelegged if your legs are in good shape. Bare legs are always sexy with high heals or sandals, (without the sun spots.) There is leg makeup that works but a great nuisance to apply as legs are large to cover.
- One friend buys bras in assorted colors so when she wears a tee it looks like it belongs together. Another friend wears only black and white. I was amazed when I looked into her closet and realized there was not one other color.

- Many women remain shopping in the junior department as clothes can be trendier and more youthful. Some women do not have missy bodies, so junior styles are best.
- Layering is very effective when your outfit seems too plain or if your shirt is a little too short, but is not flattering as a way to hide your flaws as written above. Women with white hair look amazing wearing white.
- A smart jacket is great and always in good taste especially if it is leather. I think making an investment in a great jacket or coat is worthwhile, especially if you live in cooler climates.
- Buy a classic blazer; navy blue with gold buttons, a black or white blazer. Buy an exciting hot jacket for evening; brocade, silk, white.
- Have several coats if you live in cold climate and capes are exquisite. My niece wears a fabulous grey wool cape trimmed in grey fox fur (if you are not a fur advocate) and added a rhinestone belt.
- Here are just a few great brands: James Perce tee shirts, Calypso, Ralph Lauren (always), Michaels Stars tee shirts. Shop Bloomingdales, Macy's, JCrew, Zara International, Lucky Brand Jeans, "Shop Bop" is a great web site. Much of the best is now on Amazon.com. Simply Google ex: long trendy dresses and you will find lots to compare.

WikiHow Internet site also states: You can also try these tips:

- *For a spring look, try a 1960s skirt with a matching tank, a crocheted top over it, and some pastel heels.*
- *Don't be afraid to try unique outfits…but do everyone a favor and nix the denim jacket and jeans combo!*
- *Wear colors that look good with your natural coloring.*
- *If you have a curvy figure, try outfits where you can cinch the waist with a belt. It creates the perfect hourglass figure and shows off your best features. Mine is black from the 60's and surprises me on how it enhances my body.*

- *Dress for the day and how you feel. No one wants to see someone uncomfortable in what they are wearing. Your outfit should be a reflection of your mood!*
- *Be confident smile, and be yourself.*
- *If you don't like wearing low-cut shirts, for example, layer something snug and bright under that V-neck.*
- *A black skirt goes with everything and makes an essential wardrobe staple.*

MY PERSONAL WARDROBE:

All of my clothes occupy one apartment-sized closet, with small storage in my basement to store out of season clothes and shoes.

- In my closet are three or four jackets. A red brocade, a peach silk from India, a black cut away from TJ Max, a jean jacket, a black leather coat bought in Turkey.
- Two silk suits, one in black the other in olive green bought in Vietnam.
- Three pairs of jeans.
- Two pairs of wide legged pants in white and black and many pairs of leggings (preferably black) that look great with a long blouse or shirt. A long leopard thin cotton rayon blouse.
- Two vests, one padded black, (the other two cut from jackets I no longer liked by cutting off sleeves).
- A 3/4 length white coat, a 3/4 length woven design coat. A leopard cape, a white cape, my Xmas tree cape and a twenty year old short fushsia coat that turns heads because of the color.
- One short mini suit; worn with over-the-knee boots.
- Three jumpsuits: one is black strapless, and the other is a black halter and a dark gold, several gowns for when I go on a cruise or an elaborate vacation, long dresses and skirts in black or summer colors are also great staples, (wearing bright kelly green tights and a hand painted

green tee shirt get compliments, again, because of the color.)

- Black velvet, shiny materials, a sequined black hat are amongst my favorites.
- I keep jewelry at a minimum never wanting it to over power me. I am bold enough to say I would prefer someone to admire me rather than my piece of jewelry, except for dangling earrings, even without my pierced ears. Women love jewelry and it certainly can enhance how one looks, but to me it is usually a nuisance to find in my drawer, then comes the hooking and all of my losses. There are, however two no-no's: knee-socks and silly ornaments in your hair. I leave those to thirteen-year-olds and women who live in the English countryside!

QUESTIONS FOR PERSONAL REFLECTION

1. What items in your wardrobe can you not live without? For me, it is my hooded sweatshirt. Sometimes I wear it under an elegant shawl to keep warm.
2. What are some of your fashion mistakes?
3. Do you dress with your age in mind, loving something that you think looks good on you, but feeling it my not be age appropriate?
4. Are you tempted to wear a new look but afraid that you might be laughed at by your colleagues or partner?
5. How often do you refresh your wardrobe? Have you tried to rotate your closet putting clothes out of sight for months and then bringing them back to the front of your closet?
6. Is your closet jam packed with clothes you have forgotten or with price tags still on them?
7. Would you consider giving many clothes away and having an uncluttered closet?
8. I prefer to buy where I can return just in case the store mirror or my mood was deceiving. Do you agree?

Dress to get that second look; you might be surprised at how many you get!

Notes

47

Shoes

Dear Cinderella

What can be ever so glamorous and painful at the same time? Our fabulous high heeled exciting spectacular shoes!

We girls have our own vivid memories as to when it all started; putting on mommy's shoes and playing grown up will never be forgotten.

A woman's love affair with high heeled shoes lasts for 51 years on average, with the final decision to swap to flat shoes akin to retiring from work, researchers claim.

My height was 5'3; now it is 5'2 and horrifying! Having never been tall or skinny, I have relied on high heeled shoes to make me look taller, skinner and sexier. Unfortunately, the spiked heel is no longer for me unless I'm sitting down, but then how would I be able to get up and walk? A well-known celebrity on television, about eighty years old and looking lovely after many facelifts, was helped by two men on either side as she walked to the interview chair. Perhaps no one else noticed, but she totally collapsed into the chair. She was wearing high spiked shoes and hardly made it, even with the help of two escorts.

In my era, we wore black and white saddles. Getting them dirty became a fashion statement and it was no easy task to get them perfectly filthy. Coming home that day, my sister Judy polished them as a kind sister act, much to my horror. Neither of us will ever forget the day I tormented her. We wore ballerina slippers that made us feel like dancers. Then there were penny loafers that had to be a certain soft quality so that we could easily slip a shiny penny into the slot. We slowly transitioned into spiked heels. We added rhinestone clips and buttons and for proms we dyed our shoes to match at A. S. Beck. If the color was slightly off it was unacceptable.

Today there are both flat and high heeled sneakers, classic pumps, spiked heels five and one half inches, sandals, clogs, mules, loafers, slippers, oxfords, boots of all leg and heel heights, ballerina flats, crocks, hand painted, wedged, and the list goes on and on. This year the shoes are magnificent to look at; they are works of art from shoe designers such as Jimmy Choo, Michael Kors, Chanel, Dior and many others. Any design goes—as long as you can walk in them. Regretfully, I could have been one of those designers, having designed the first decorative sneaker back in the early 1980s. I had bought shoe material in gold and silver sequins and metal bindings and sat in my apartment for months decorating sneakers. At the time my design was so innovative that I feared somebody would steal the idea, so I literally hid them under my bed. I could not find a way to market them, and there is no protection for design, so it slid by. A sorry story, as it became one of the biggest industries in sneaker transformation using the same material and styling as mine, and taught me a good lesson on fear and sharing.

The funniest pair of shoes I ever had were Steve Maddens high wedged silver sparkling shoes with Lucite straps. One evening, when wearing the ten year old shoes out, one seemed lower than another. As the evening wore on, it seemed that the shoes were slowly disintegrating. I realized I was getting lower and lower until the shoes collapsed to the ground. They were made with some sort of foam, and there I was, walking on the bare soles rather than 4" platforms. It was truly hilarious.

Sketchers makes great sneaker shoes that go through thick and thin without wearing out under the worst of circumstances. They do not mind going through mud, rocks, water, or you name it.

Medically as we get older, our spines change form and we do not balance our bodies in the same way. In these years wedged heels are for me. Finally shoe designers have recognized that most women cannot wear a spiked heel throughout their lives. Wedged heels came into style briefly in the early nineties and I cherished the ones I bought back then. On a trip to Hawaii one of my wedged shoes was lost. Feeling fearful that I would never find a replacement or wear high heels again, I combed the island for the lost shoe, but I never found it. It took a while for designers to bring back the wedge, but now they are bigger than ever. The wedged shoe gives support that a stiletto cannot. However, I do have one friend who is eighty plus who walks the city wearing stiletto heels every day (which to me is incredible). Not only can she wear them, she states to my amazement:

"I feel more comfortable in spikes than in flats."

"Shoes can make your day," says my daughter-in-law. "Give a girl the right shoes and she can conquer the world," said Marilyn Monroe. Women and men both love to see a woman in high heels. Women remember first shoes more than the first kiss. Then, for the intimate moments, what is more sexy than wearing high heeled shoes to bed and having your lover take them off one by one? Or as we've seen in a recent Broadway show, having a man lift your leg gently, put on a knee-high boot, and zip it up slowly?

So who invented high heels? High heels actually came to be in the 15th century. It was used to help horsemen have a better footing in the stirrups of their horses. Over time it became a more fashion-oriented trend among men. It helped to differentiate nobility and status from all the rest. Then about 30 years after the first heels were invented, a woman named Catherine de Medici who was the wife of the Duke of Orleans got a cobbler to fashion her a pair of these heels to help define her status. It pretty much goes on from there. As you can see women are predominately the ones who now wear heels. To this day almost all women own at least one pair of heels. Not for status of nobility, but for a status of being "the desired."

High heels are uncomfortable and make walking more difficult. Prolonged use can injure the feet, knees and back. So why do women keep wearing them?

The short answer seems to be that women in heels are more likely to attract favorable notice.

In Sense and Sensibility, *Jane Austen describes the character Elinor Dashwood as having a "delicate complexion, regular features, and remarkably good figure." But Austen describes Elinor's sister, Marianne, as "still handsomer. Her form, though not so correct as her sister's, in having the advantage of height, was more striking."*

Along with making women taller, high heels force the back to arch, pushing the bosom forward and the buttocks rearward, thus accentuating the female form.

"Men like an exaggerated female figure," writes fashion historian Caroline Cox. The problem is that if all women wear high heels, such advantages tend to cancel out. Height, after all, is a relative phenomenon. It may be advantageous to be taller than others, or at

least not to be several inches shorter. But when all wear shoes that make them several inches taller, the relative height distribution is unaffected, so no one appears taller than if all had worn flat heels. … the height of the heels she chooses is also a reflection of the ups and downs of her life, varying drastically from teenage years to motherhood and old age. The passion for higher fashion begins at the age of 12, and continues through every stage of a woman's life until she reaches 63, says the report, which was compiled by High Street fashion store Debenhams.

Only advancing age and increasing frailty finally brings the enduring love affair to a reluctant end, the figures show. Debenham's spokesman Ed Watson said that the psychological effect of retiring from heels can be almost as traumatic as retiring from work." It's an all-too-public admission that they are getting older, and so naturally many women want to postpone this evil day for as long as possible," he said.

"Nevertheless, there comes a time when women have to admit that, while they may still feel young, in practice, they're not as steady on their feet as they once were. 'It's a climb down which can cause much heartache.'"

Debenhams undertook its research as part of an extensive examination of the entire women's shoe market.

"However, despite our findings, we feel certain that there are still many elderly women who still insist in stepping out in super high heels, defying age to trip them up. 'If so, we'd love to hear from them. Finding out what all of our customers want to wear, regardless of age, is the secret of success in retail.'"

For me, I noticed early on wearing a black dress with black shoes was not appealing to me unless worn with black stockings; even so, black clothes with black shoes never looked good, even though it has always been a popular style. Wearing a contrasting shoe looked much better when wearing black, but it was a not until recent years that it was in Vogue. The head shoe buyer at Saks Fifth Avenue, Betty Davis states, "Nude color shoes make a longer leg and create an illusion of a super long leg."

Contrasting shoes look great with black dresses, worn with white, red, silver or gold shoes. My lime green summer blouse and pants with red wedged shoes and a red necklace look great. We can all be creative, as almost anything goes.

I have now learned to carry an extra pair of shoes with me, starting out in flats and bringing heels or starting out in heels and bringing flats.

"This also preserves your heels, and with the high cost of designer shoes, protects your investment," Ms. Davis states.

There is nothing worse than feet that hurt and the longing to get home and kick off the shoes you loved a few hours earlier. How many times has it seemed impossible to make it home walking in bare or stocking feet because of the pain? Then there was the delightful experience of running barefoot through the streets of NYC, jumping into puddles with shoes in hand having been caught in a severe rainstorm. Another shoe story is about my friend who went to an eloquent New Year's Eve party wearing a gorgeous new pair of spiked shoes. Upon arrival, the door was opened by a butler and as she made her grand entrance she completely slid on the floor landing on her back side.

My grandmother had feet that hurt her, so she chose to wear oxford lace up shoes in whites or cream colors. When she was in her late seventies she met a man who loved her and wanted to marry her. However, he begged her to wear different shoes, as he felt her lace up oxfords with a square loafer heal were very unbecoming to her. She refused.

"These are the shoes I wear."

The story goes that he married another woman. Now you might say, "What a shallow man." Not having met him, from what I am told, he was a man who loved beautiful women from head to toe. Don't get me wrong—I love sneakers when I work out or walk and flats look great too, but there I am—back to my 5' 2" plus. It is often said, that even if you cannot buy a new outfit, put on a pair of sexy shoes and no one will care what else you are wearing.

Princess Margaret gave up wearing high heels—her way of announcing to the world that she was getting older. She died soon afterwards. While it is difficult to wear high heels for the reasons mentioned above, put them on at least occasionally. Don't ever give them up. If in the end we collapse, might as well be wearing our high heels!

QUESTIONS FOR PERSONAL REFLECTION:

1. Have you reached a point where comfort is far more important to you than being taller?
2. Do you have a favorite pair of shoes that you will never part with?
3. Do you have a personal memory of a wonderful pair of shoes and the time you had wearing them?
4. If you are built tall and slim do you enjoy wearing high heeled shoes to be even taller?
5. Zappos is a great shoe site. Nordstrom is also great for shoes. Do you order from either? Some people feel shoes and bags should be expensive, wanting to sport designer labels. To me, cost does not matter; I like what looks good on me.

Notes

48

Facelifts:

Have You Tried One On Yet?

Florence Lipman, my darling mom, wrote at 82 years old, "I don't have space for more wrinkles on my face"

Do you believe in plastic surgery? If you asked me that question, I would say, " Absolutely, sign me up."

I believe in facelifts, eye lifts, lasers, peels, Botox, Restylane, anything that keeps my face upward and my skin clear. Here is to the confident and incredible plastic surgeon, skilled enough to open my face and then put it back together again, taking years off my life. Here is to the scientist who can soothe away wrinkles enough for me to enjoy a refreshed look, and "who can make more space for more wrinkles on my face." I have had many cosmetic procedures. Everyone has different monetary values. Cosmetic surgery is my extravagance and I save my money for this purpose.

Thrifty in other ways, but not when it comes to wrinkles, pouches, and bags, they simply do not look well on my face. Running for help each time there is a flaw is not what I do, but somehow my face knows when it's time. Most procedures are spaced with intervals of about five years. Now we are blessed with "Liquid Facelifts"... Restylane, Perlane, Radiesse, Juvederm, Artefill, Sculpto and of course Botox which have saved many from going through surgery.

At forty-two my first procedure was to remove the bags under my eyes. I believe that the breakup of my marriage, around that time, caused the bags under my eyes to be more pronounced. I heard about Dr. MacDonald from my dermatologist. Driving into NYC from New Jersey, I arrived at his upper Fifth Avenue eerie office. It was dimly lit and extremely quiet and nobody else was in the waiting room. It was all so secretive. He had a lovely nurse who made my trembling knees stop shaking. She escorted me into his office. He was a tall, thin man and his delicate hands and long fine fingers were immediately noticed.

Telling him why I was there made me feel shy and embarrassed, admitting that there was something inferior about me. It was at a different time when plastic surgery and psychotherapy were shameful. He of course thought the procedure would be an improvement; it was a go.

The day of surgery, at Roosevelt Hospital in New York City, I was a physical wreck worrying, "Suppose he distorts my face, or blinds me?" My tremendous fears, bordered on crazy. Who would not be terrified, going in for the first time, without knowing anybody who had done the procedure and only having read about it in magazines. Dr. MacDonald was kind and gentle and seemed to have taken a liking to my insecurities. My eyes came out to perfection. He said it would take a week or two to heal. It took me one month. I think everyone heals at a different pace, Yet there was no question that I looked refreshed and renewed and those terrible bags were gone. If a person has only one cosmetic surgery make it the balsectomy as it will take away the tired look that bags create. Pouches make us look old and tired.

Ten years later, it was time for a facelift. It was not that my skin was hanging or such, but there was a change and wanted to take care of it before anyone else noticed. Back to Dr. MacDonald, again petrified, even more so than the first time; now it was my whole face at risk. After checking into Roosevelt Hospital in New York City again, in the early morning my fears got hold of me and placed a call to the doctor telling him I was too afraid to go through with it. My crazy frightened feelings had returned and I would have done anything to evacuate. He calmed me down, telling me it will be all right, and by the end of the conversation, I was ready. Suddenly, I had a new fear—that I had awakened him from his sleep and maybe he had not gotten the right amount of rest to perform the operation. Lying on the operating table under anesthesia, I heard him say,

"She has little to take away and she will look fantastic." I guess he could see the results, before the swelling set in. Lying there, with absolutely no pain, bored, wanting to get up, realizing why they strapped me in so tightly. There was a story of a woman named Ivy, who did sit up on the operating table, causing her doctor to scream out with horror. Dr. MacDonald only did a little here and a little here. To me, it made a difference, but no one else seemed to notice, which had both good and bad points; I looked natural but I still wanted someone to notice how great I looked.

There is no pain attached to having a facelift. However, it is uncomfortable, especially to lie flat rather than on your side, if that is your position. My surgeries are well paced with careful decisions on the doctor chosen. It is not about the money or how famous the doctor is; it's about how he perceives me as a person. Many times we are just a number to a doctor who has countless patients, so I make sure the doctor knows that Carol Sue Gershman is being wheeled into the operating room. This is achieved by getting the doctor's attention by going back frequently and complaining.

"Are you sure I need it now? Is it going to go well?

"Suppose you do not get the right amount of rest, the night before, and your hand is tired?" In other words, I become a pest with humor and this has worked well. I ask many questions and see him often before surgery asking questions that are related. By the time surgery came, it was most certain the doctor knew exactly who was being rolled in.

Living in Florida, driving my car in the sun, plus age, began to put many brown spots and wrinkles on my face. A procedure called "Younger Face" was introduced to me by Dr. Lucy. She was educated in South America and swore to the serum she brought back with her from her country. She had an excellent facial salon where she told me how beautiful my skin would look with her procedure. Her patients looked excellent and were all calm and peaceful when it was over as she invited me to meet them. The procedure she said, would entail me staying with her the first night, when she would prepare my face. I would sleep, completely bandaged, in discomfort, but not pain. A nurse would watch over me, all through the night. For the next eight days, I would remain in bed, lying with my face straight up on a pillow. Each day, she would visit me, adding her magical formula, which was some sort of powder that soothed the skin over the hardened mask and stopped the itching and discomfort. At the end of eight days, she said I would have the skin of a newborn and look ten years younger. At the same time, laser was becoming the thing. Dr. Geronomos in New York City was the top man in this department. The laser machine would burn off layers of my skin leaving it like a baby's. It was the latest discover in smoothing wrinkles. Dr. Lucy's procedure seemed to be a waste of time. Convincing myself to forget about the secret formula and to go the laser route, the morning of surgery, the doctor wanted to know how I was. I responded by saying,

"I am just fine, but more important, how are you?"

It was a horrible thing to go through, much worse than any facelift. It was over in perhaps an hour's time but the week ahead was gruesome. I looked like I had been in a fire. It was painful and ice had to be applied constantly. Round-the-clock nurses the first two nights were necessary and it was slow to heal. It took more than the usual time for me but soon enough my skin was magical and kept me happy for the next five years.

For my second facelift, I connected with a woman from Miami Beach who had a well known facial salon and was adamant about a plastic surgeon in Peru. She had been flying in and out, over the years, to have a little something here and a little something there removed at a fraction of the cost she would have to pay in the States. She organized a group every August, arranging all the details and receiving a commission from the doctor for her services, which would pay for her own surgery. One August, I decided to join her group of five women who wanted to look better. One lady was a nurse, another was a housewife and another was an attorney. We landed in Lima, around midnight, and went straight to the doctor's office, where he met all of us together for the first time. I was to pay up front and be operated on the next morning. He gave the same interview to everybody, and he frightened me right out of his office to start a search for another surgeon. This is what I always avoided—a doctor who didn't know me and who would do what he does to everyone, without a personal touch on any level. The group hated me for stepping away, as they all moved forward, especially the lady who put it together, as she had just lost her commission. I decided to do research on my own while

I was in Peru. Lima was known for plastic surgeons. There were many and one was cheaper than the other compared to the states. Each day, I went out to seek a new doctor; like a job, going to work unable to reach a decision.

Meanwhile, back at the hotel that had been booked for my two week stay, the group isolated me, not letting me join their cutup, bandaged faces at dinner treating me as a rebel and an outcast. I was trying to make a decision on what to do, disappointed that I could not make one with another doctor and hoping I had not made a mistake by not having it done with the original doctor. My son was about to be married and his wedding was my motivation for having it done at all. I decided to take a break from it all, going to Machu Picchu to pray to the gods to help me make the right decision. They told me to go back to the States.

When I returned a friend suggested a Dr. Somers in Miami Beach. I waited for hours in his office to meet him and almost left. Finally he carefully evaluated my face, telling me what he thought would be best. I could see he was conservative and would do little as possible, leaving me to look natural, with the least amount of scarring. He was the right doctor for me, kind, handsome and honest. He performed the operation in his office, set up as a clinic and had tender-loving care for my two-day stay. It was perfect!

My mom always said before each procedure,

"Oh darling, you don't need it."

Then she would look at me post-op and tell me it was a good idea.

About ten years later, I decided it was time to do try Dr. Lucy's, "Younger Face." I called several of Doctor Lucy's patients for their final critique as she had suggested taking the local bus to her clinic. Several hours later, there I was, immobile and completely bandaged. When she removed the partial bandage the next morning I had grotesque white stuff on my face with my two red eyes peering out, and looking like a monster. She said I was ready to go home.

I wasn't allowed to talk, the doctor not wanting my lip movements to change a thing, in fear that one of the wrinkles would reappear; so, I lay silent, waiting each day for the doctor to return and apply her magic serum. Each day she was late.

My face itched, it stung, and the powder puffed me out, making me look more hideous. It was not painful, simply uncomfortable. I was able to watch TV; Hurricane Katrina had hit New Orleans, making the city a heck of a lot scarier than me. On the eighth day, Dr. Lucy arrived earlier than usual because the mask was ready to come off. It was an exciting morning. She slowly removed everything, wiping and cleaning my skin. In a few more moments, I would be able to look in the mirror. In retrospect, those days went by very quickly and it was a good rest. The nicest part of this procedure is that I was able to immediately go out and start my younger life. I slowly walked to the mirror, fearing to look. When I did, what I saw was a red face. My skin was beautiful and smooth with not a mark on it. It seemed that everything had been lifted as well. My eyes looked good and my cheekbones seemed to be up farther. Dr. Lucy called out,

"How do you like it? How do you like it? I told you, it would be good."

"Yes, I think I look different, but it's difficult to tell, if I have changed for the good or bad."

"You look fabulous, at least ten, maybe fifteen, years younger."

Generally, these procedures are excellent, but nothing truly lasts. The surgery is good for a while, but the aging continues when we leave the operating table. We can get a few good years each time, and never have to see ourselves looking old and sagging. The day might come where it won't work any more and hope that that day doesn't come any time soon. The wonderful news is that now there is always something new on the market and going under the knife as they say, may be obsolete in the future.

One of my friends waited until she was seventy-five. Perhaps she was frightened or did not want to spend the money. Finally looking older than her years with much sagging she decided to have her face lifted. When she came out I noticed a drastic change. She looked kinder, happier and beautiful. For most of us nature takes its course, facelifts do make us feel better about ourselves.

SOME RECOMMENDATIONS FOR YOU

- Be ready. Know that you are doing this to feel better about yourself.

- Carefully choose the right doctor, not one your friends like, one that you like. This is personal stuff. Visit three.

- Know that you will look better, cleaner, clearer but please do not expect to look twenty years younger. Up to ten is a great wish.

- If you are way overweight, lose the weight before you go in. A few pounds will not make any difference.

- Be a good patient, do what your doctor tells you to do to heal correctly; don't be in a rush and enjoy the process.

- Be informed to what is available now, such as less invasive lasers. New procedures are constantly hitting the market.

QUESTIONS FOR PERSONAL REFLECTION

1. Are you considering a facelift?
2. How many have you had? Are you looking well enough without getting another one?
3. Would you consider going to another country to save money, keeping in mind that if anything goes wrong you are far from home?
4. Once the sad looking angry lines are gone, you will look refreshed with a new outlook on life. It might not change how you feel about yourself, but it sure will change your face and for the better.

Notes

49

Posture

Sit Up Straight, What's Down There Anyway?

Now you have adorned yourself in every possibly way, you have struggled to diet, you are slim, your hair has never looked better and you're wearing clothes that become you. No more sloppy big baggy pants with a large tee covering up your new body. You are looking good and feeling good about yourself and you are ready to step out. You meet a friend for dinner who notices the wonderful changes you have made, but when you sit down, you suddenly slump in your chair changing your entire aura, and "The New and Amazing You" you have accomplished. A woman with good posture sits tall, walks tall, her stomach held in, and her head is always held high. A woman does not lean on a table unless she is looking into someone's eyes.

A person who slouches looks uncomfortable and no doubt feels uncomfortable. How do I know? Because I have poor posture because of my back in my yoga and pilates classes. The poses where I am asked to sit with crossed legs on a mat are very uncomfortable for me, so I slouch which hurts my back and spine. On the days that I happen to be more flexible it is a great feeling to sit up tall on my mat. Otherwise good posture is something I am aware of; trying to carry myself upright. If you know you slump and practice poor posture, constantly remind yourself to sit up tall or ask a friend to remind you.

In dance classes the instructor tells his students, "It is important to maintain good posture by not looking at your feet; look up straight, smile and don't worry about your step."

I was fortunate to have a mom who would say, "Sit up," when I was slouching.

QUESTIONS FOR PERSONAL REFLECTION

1. Are you aware of your own posture or that of those around you?
2. If you have back problems, would wearing a brace help you to have better posture?
3. Have you been tempted to tell someone, "Sit up straight, you are slouching."
4. Has anyone ever told you that you are slouching? Are you aware of your own posture or that of those around you?
5. Walking tall is just as important as sitting tall. When you walk down the street are your shoulders held high?

Be proud of who you are; walk and sit tall.

Notes

50

Vanity

Go Ahead And Be Your Old Vain Self

Whether it be manicures, posture, sleep, teeth, facelifts, makeup or hair we all need a bit of vanity to make it all come true.

If you are not vain, or place little importance on how you look you will ultimately let yourself go and both your health and beauty may start to decline.

I have said many times over that nature does not care and one day you might look in the mirror and say, "What happened to me?" Taking pride in yourself is a gift to you and there is a big difference between being vain or being conceited even though both words are readily confused.

Being vain to me is what I learned from my family. Their day would begin with a shower and then immediately getting dressed even if they were going to stay home. After breakfast the makeup went on and the nails polished and they were ready for visitors, work or errands.

For those of us who work at home, it is easy to look sloppy around the house. We are anxious to begin the day of work, not bothering to dress. But it will make a big difference to how you feel if you do. By all means get out of those pajamas and robe.

Vanity is taking pride in yourself and showing the world that you care about you. It is not being conceited, which ties in with your ego which might make you feel above the next person, jealous or selfish. It is essentially important to be vain in everything you do; your looks, your work.

SOME RECOMMENDATIONS FOR YOU:

- Take the time to check yourself each day. If you see something that needs beautifying or better version of you, do it.
- You never know who you might run into it at any given moment. When that occurs, it is a great feeling knowing you are looking well. On the same note, you never know who is watching you.
- Looking into the mirror occasionally to check how you look is vanity/pride. Looking into every passing mirror is being conceited.

QUESTIONS FOR SELF REFLECTION

1. Do you consider yourself to be a vain person by taking pride in how you look?
2. Do you not bother with yourself if nobody is around to see you?
3. Are your friends envious or judgmental hoping to find a flaw in you, judging you on your looks?

Don't let anyone or anything get in the way of your vanity.

Notes

Epilogue

Peggy Lee must have had her own reasons for singing the plaintive tune, "Is That All There Is," but we don't have to see life that way. There are bundles of joy ahead for each of us when we live passionately, make new discoveries, see other points of view, reinvent ourselves with a new talent or vocation and make our dreams come true. Perhaps Ms. Lee, might have said, is that all the time there is?

Some people are truly happy with themselves and their lifestyle and bravo to them as there is nothing better. Keep your spirt alive and growing, refreshing yourself with water and kindness and watch how life can grow in ways you never thought possible.

It is important not to live with any regrets. It does not matter at what point of life a new adventure, accomplishment, love comes to you as long as you get it in your lifetime. Don't let anyone step in the way of a new idea you are excited about achieving. Your friends mean well but some simply may not know how to get out of their own box.

Health is number one, as it is hard to do anything without it. Exercise and whip yourself into good shape and stay at a good healthy weight. Keep the fun alive in you that is God-given, but take baby steps in living an ageless and passionate life, taking anything new one step at a time. There is time for everything, especially a good time—and I might add that we all spell a good time differently. A good time to me now might be writing or speaking rather than partying. Surely there are many ways that you spell a good time.

Finally, treat yourself royally for the day, then a week, then a year. Don't you think we all need to take some time for ourselves in this extremely fast paced and busy world? Each day belongs to you. Go out and make fabulous stories. That is what our lives are; one big and brilliant story. Let yours become bigger, better, healthier, happier, sexier and more vibrant! An exciting woman is an exciting woman at any age, and for the few good men reading this, ditto!

About the Author

Carol Sue Gershman attended the Miami Dade College memoir class in 2007 thoughtfully morphing her two and a half page story "Adventure in Love" into her first book, *The Jewish Woman, The Black Man and The Road Trip*. She states: "Who knew by going on a romantic road trip adventure I would be destined to become an author?"

She has been asked, *What differentiates you from other authors who write books to help better society?* "Well, I must admit I am the oldest living author out there! Therefore at age 77, I have more experience."

Her main goal is to inspire women and a few men to live a life that will fulfill their hopes and dreams at any age.

Here Comes Amazing You is written in five parts, taking the reader through topics that are most familiar to them. It has taken two years to write, research and edit. Why forty-nine ideas? "I started out with 74 ideas, then it went to 60, then 54 and when it was down to 49 ideas I had not one more thing to say. She also states that the 50th and best idea is in you.

Carol Sue Gershman enjoys living life by reinventing herself on a constant level. She now lives in NYC having enjoyed the phenomenon of South Beach Miami life for eighteen years. She has 3 children and 5 grandchildren. Her favorite projects are writing, singing, traveling, exercising, dating and hardly has enough time in each day to fulfill her own hopes and dreams. "Then again maybe I have. Writing may be it!"

Contact:

Carol Sue Gershman
212-874-4194
carolsue11@yahoo.com

CPSIA information can be obtained at www.ICGtesting.com
Printed in the USA
BVOW030454190413

318566BV00001B/4/P